WAY DOWN
in
UPPER EGYPT

WAY DOWN
in
UPPER EGYPT

An intimate look at a western woman's life
in villages along the Nile.

Jonna Castle

author HOUSE®

AuthorHouse™ LLC
1663 Liberty Drive
Bloomington, IN 47403
www.authorhouse.com
Phone: 1-800-839-8640

Published by AuthorHouse   06/26/2013

ISBN: 978-1-4817-5862-8 (sc)
ISBN: 978-1-4817-5861-1 (hc)
ISBN: 978-1-4817-5863-5 (e)

Library of Congress Control Number: 2013910006

Contents

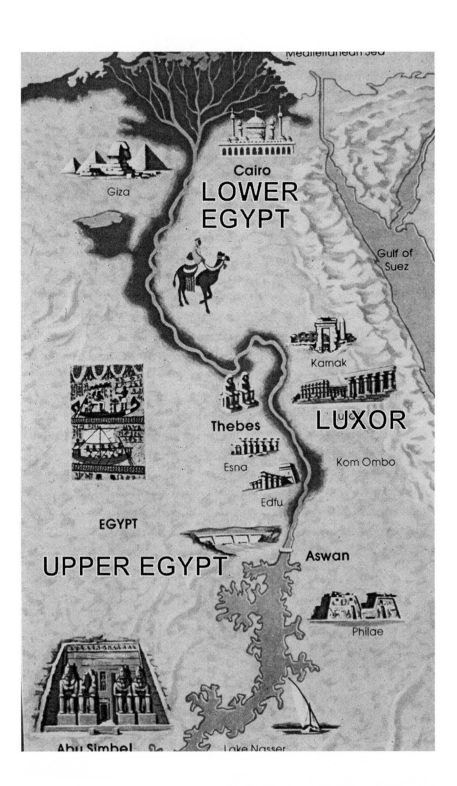

Introduction

I used to live in Egypt. I told all my little friends that. To my kindergarten and early childhood friends, there was nothing unusual about it and this was perfectly accepted. Yet, not one of us had any idea of where or what Egypt was. It was clear to me that I had a previous life there and I never questioned it. I just assumed that everyone felt this way. There were many memories, including sitting on the smooth rocks beside the swiftly flowing water and watching the boats go by. My memory is very vividly filled with one particular boat that was larger than all the rest and was much prettier than the other boats. It had gold trim on it but I didn't know the significance of gold at my young age. I remember it because the sun shining on the gold caused me to squint and cover my eyes. This boat had many men at the oars and its sail was the largest on the river. Sometimes I could hear music coming from this boat.

I can still envision some of my playmates running and playing along the river banks in the tall flowering grass that grew higher than our heads. This green plant was fascinating because the strong thick stalk was not round. It was three-sided and that made it feel odd in my hand. It grew as far as the eye could see. Many years later I learned that this plant is called papyrus and it was used liberally in previous times; as a writing material; also woven into sandals, mats, animal cages and sun shades, just to name a few. Maybe that explains why it is now extinct in the wild in Egypt.

The sharpness and some details of those memories have now faded. When little children tell me about their fantasy world and their world of make believe, I stop to listen and then encourage them to talk about it. For this may not be a fantasy at all, but rather a very distant memory.

There is another delightful memory. I recall anxiously thinking that I must hurry and grow up so that I can go to Egypt and see the pyramids. After all, my six-year-old mind reasoned, they are already over four thousand years old and they might fall down before I can go there to see them. Well, as children tend to do, I did hurry and grow up, the pyramids did not fall down and I have had the rich pleasure of visiting them, inside and out, many times.

So began my love affair with present day Egypt. We are told there is a time for everything under heaven, and many years passed before it was my time to return to Egypt. Education, marriage, children, homemaking and career all had their time before I could go back to the land that I call home.

Over the years I became busy with life but never lost my interest in Egypt. I had an opportunity to become a docent at the 1987 Egyptian traveling exhibit, Ramses II, The Great Pharaoh and His Time. That meant seriously studying about Ancient Egypt—something more than just reading an occasional book.

I could not get enough. It became an addiction. Sometimes I felt like I was reading my own biography. Nearly everything seemed familiar. It was like discovering me. Common names and certain ancient words came to me very easily. Places were recognizable. I could not know enough. Even after the five and a half-month run of the exhibit, I still could not stop studying.

There were others who shared my passion for learning about ancient Egypt and we often studied together and shared our information. We ultimately formed a group called The Egyptian Study Society (ESS). This organization thrives today, over twenty years later.

When the first century historian Herodotus visited this country he wrote that Egypt is the gift of the Nile. How true. The only arable land extends about two to fifteen miles on either side of this mighty river. The majority of Egypt's eighty-six million people live on the banks of the Nile, creating one of the highest population densities in the world. Without the River Nile, Egypt would be simply an uninhabitable desert.

In 1995 I was making my fifth trip to this mystical land and decided I had enough funds to live there comfortably for three months. I had just dissolved a long-term marriage, the children were grown and on their own, and I needed time alone to think about my future. Little did I know that this three month visit would develop into a life-changing three year residency.

Previous trips could be called study trips but this time I wanted to simply relax, observe more about the current culture, the religion, practice the language, all while continuing my studies.

In ancient times Egypt was divided into Upper and Lower Egypt, and it carries the same designation today. New Kingdom pharaohs wore crowns of a different shape and color for Upper Egypt and Lower Egypt. Sometimes the two crowns were combined and worn together, thus forming one unique crown for Egypt, the united land.

Upper Egypt is in the southern or higher part of the country. Lower Egypt is in the northern or lower part of Egypt. Looking at a map, the country appears to be turned upside down. This is because the River Nile, the longest river in the world (just over four thousand miles), flows from East Africa north to the Mediterranean Sea. It actually cuts Egypt into two parts, creating the eastern desert and the western desert.

Ancient Thebes, now known as modern Luxor, is an incredible area for pharaonic era statuary, temples and tombs. It is called the largest outdoor museum of antiquities in the world; therefore it is a tourist destination. Despite its popularity, Upper Egypt remains ultra-conservative, very poor, has a high illiteracy rate, and many

Egyptians even label this area as backward and far behind the times. Here they faithfully honor the old ways.

Having the opportunity to live for a number of years in this region, and become a part of a large family and experience the rich village life is unique and richly rewarding. For the next twenty-five years I divided my time between Egypt and my home country, the USA—each year adding additional months to my time in this desert land. I had the opportunity to live in different areas of Luxor, and on both sides of the Nile. This introduced me to the modern anthropology of Upper Egypt—if anything in this part of the world can be called modern.

Daily life was an exciting challenge. It seems that everything ended with a story to tell. As I told my friends about my life's experiences, they continuously said, "You should write a book." I just laughed at that idea as I continued my exciting journey. After my mother died I discovered that she had saved every letter I had written to her from Egypt and each letter served as a journal and a reminder, complete with dates and names and many things that had since left my memory. What a treasure my mother provided for me.

Foreword

The town of Luxor is rather small and poor—at least by most western standards. It is not the grand city it was when it was known as Thebes, the capital of New Kingdom Egypt, nearly four thousand years ago. My imagination knows no boundaries when I visualize all the palaces and grand and glorious homes that we know were there in times past.

My first home was a rented apartment in the conservative town of Luxor, and then later I lived in a lovely desert home in the rural area of the west bank, where many of the places I wanted to learn more about were located. Never having been to the residential or business areas of Luxor, I knew no one in the town. Previous visits to this area always found me staying in the five-star hotels beside the Nile, far removed from mixing and mingling with the Egyptian people.

This is a collection of personal experiences I had with the local farmers, drivers, waiters, housewives, children, fishermen and boatmen, even strangers—everyone I met over this extended period of time.

Most of the names of individuals in my stories have been changed due to cultural sensitivity—especially for the women—but every incident is true and factual. What you read here about the customs of Upper Egypt will not always coincide with other areas of this magnificent country, particularly the metropolitan areas of Cairo and Alexandria.

The pace of Upper Egypt remains very slow and old fashioned and, yes maybe a little backward.

Today, coming off the airplane, and placing my feet on Egyptian soil, I feel as if I have finally arrived home again. My blood pulsates through my veins. My breath temporarily leaves me. It's quite an emotional time for me, and yes, the tears come. When a total stranger singles me out on the city streets, and says, "Welcome home, my sister," I know I am where I belong.

Welcome to My Egypt

I wasn't even unpacked or settled into my first flat when a small group of neighborhood children timidly knocked on my door—I'd guess their average age was twelve years. They came to welcome me but I sensed that they were just curious and wanted to look me over; this flat had not been occupied for four years.

I invited them in, showed them around and let them know that the water had not yet been turned on; therefore I could not cook, clean up, wash dishes, bathe, or flush the toilet. Then I gave each child a large empty container and each one ran gleefully away to fill up his container with water and return to me. This was my introduction to my new neighborhood.

The children came every day and usually brought me some item of special food from their home and their mother—a loaf of freshly baked bread or sweets. Then in keeping with Egyptian custom, they inquired daily, "Do you need anything? Do you want anything?" This is a question that is on everyone's lips. As he leaves the house in the morning, a husband always asks his wife this. Family members phone other family members before bedtime to make this inquiry. Friends question each other along with their good-byes.

I knew the children were reporting back to their mothers who reported to the other neighborhood women. Every woman for blocks now was aware of all my trials and tribulations and that's exactly the way I wanted it. Now the invitations were arriving from the mothers and grandmothers, aunts and cousins. I was invited for tea, lunch, or dinner nearly every day and it became necessary to keep a social calendar. They wanted to look me over and I wanted to know all about them, so it was a rewarding exchange.

The laptop was unheard of because computers were not yet available in Luxor, but I had brought a word processor with me and I let the children use it to do their English lessons. They were thrilled! They had never seen anything like that! So we had a mutual exchange going. They took care of me and I took care of them—to some extent.

I was quickly drawn into the life of the neighborhood and was included in the neighborhood news and gossip. Everyone was patient and helpful with my limited Arabic. No one spoke English. At that time there were only a half-dozen western women living in the town of Luxor, but not in our neighborhood, so I was a bit of a novelty. As I walked in the streets, women leaned over their high brick and cement balconies and called down to me, "Is your friend feeling better today?" Or maybe, "You had a guest this afternoon. I told her you would return home around this time." I felt as if I belonged. More important, I felt as if I was being taken care of.

Here in Upper Egypt the culture differs significantly from the rest of the country and it is unique to experience life here, quite the same as it was lived a hundred or two hundred years ago. Upper Egypt has stood still in time.

One evening as I sat in a small kiosk in the *suq* (market place) waiting for a broken piece of luggage to be repaired, I looked at the window and saw a half dozen of my neighborhood children jumping up and down outside, trying to get my attention, and each holding up five fingers. I got the message immediately and once I smiled and nodded a silent "yes," they went on their way.

Merchants usually charge tourists at least twice as much as they charge locals, and the children were telling me how much I should pay. Here in Upper Egypt it's called tourist price and Egyptian price and it is a factor in almost everything, from renting a flat to buying a loaf of bread. They didn't want me to be overcharged. After some bartering and haggling, the repairman accepted five Egyptian pounds, down from a starting rate of fifteen Egyptian. *Ilhamdu lil Allah,* (thanks to God), just as the children indicated. Bless them.

The children became my best source of information and my best language teachers. I was always amazed at how creative and clever they were at teaching me Arabic words I needed to know. Often there was a lot of theatrics involved. One day they asked me if there was too much *dousha.* When they determined that I didn't know that word, they got into a huddle and had a quiet whispered conversation with one another, and then they suddenly began speaking very loudly, all at the same time. Of course, it didn't take much to figure out that *dousha* means noise and I never forgot that word. They spoke no English. The English they were learning from their textbook was definitely not conversational. They were adorable and patient.

Sewing for the
Egyptian Women

Little did I know at the time that Egypt would be my home for the next three years. Once I determined that I would be in Luxor for a while, I faced another hurdle: it was necessary that I support myself, yet my visa said employment was not permitted and there were no jobs for foreign women who spoke limited Arabic.

I had been a professional seamstress, quilt maker and textile artist for about twenty years, so I did what seemed sensible and logical for me in this situation; I simply purchased a sewing machine and went into business sewing for the Egyptian women. I quickly learned a new Arabic vocabulary to include sewing related words, learned to work in the metric system, learned to barter hard and quick, and I met and sewed for many of the town's best dressed women.

The style at that time involved wearing two piece suits for women and these women were very proud to have their suits made by a western seamstress. It seemed a perfect match as I also have a good tailoring background. Most tailors in Egypt are men and a man must never touch a woman's body, or even get close, or take a serious look. So he can't fit her properly. I had some flyers made up emphasizing "western style clothing made by a skilled western woman." I felt it was very important to emphasize "western" as this implied a certain style and higher quality.

Too, there was a lot of prestige associated with having a western woman sewing for an Egyptian woman and I wanted them to expect only the best.

I was very excited when my first Egyptian customer arrived—a nice figure and pretty young lady. I surmised she would be good advertising for one of my Western style suits. I could not believe my ears when she placed her order. She wanted a belly dancing costume. I declined, saying that I had never made such a garment and wouldn't know how to begin. This professional dancer simply smiled that special Egyptian way, looked me straight in the eye and with that odd little grin on her lips, said, "Yes, I know. That is why I came to you. I want something different."

Now, a belly dancing costume is definitely not in keeping with the rules of dressing in the Muslim world. While women wear lose fitting dresses because they do not want to display body curvature, a dancing costume exposes much more than it covers. The belly, hips and breasts must be seen as they are the body parts most often in motion. That leaves little to cover. A dancer's costume is beaded and glittery so that attention is called to these moving areas of her body.

Together we collaborated on design and I made her a costume that was a little more modest than she was accustomed to. She seemed very pleased to have a one-of-a-kind garment and especially one that concealed a little more than she usually kept under wraps. However, she was back in my workroom within two weeks, requesting that I make another one, exactly like the first one. It seems someone else liked it also, as it was stolen from the club where she was performing.

Sayeed and Jamalat

His English vocabulary probably did not exceed one hundred words. As his vocabulary grew, so did our friendship. I met Sayeed on the ferry that carries residents back and forth from the town of Luxor on the east side of the Nile River to the west side. The west is an agricultural area populated by small villages of *fellahin* (farmers and peasants), a distance of about a half mile directly across the Nile. It was 1989 during my first trip to Egypt. I had that odd feeling that *I knew this man*—that we had met before—but of course, that was not possible.

Sayeed and his young family lived in a one room mud brick house in the tiny village of Biryat, on the west side of the Nile. As I visited Egypt regularly during the coming years, I spent much of my time with Sayeed, the head of this group. He was a sort of self-styled guide, although he knew absolutely nothing of Egypt's ancient past. But he knew the name of everyone in his village and he could recite every family's history. He could identify every growing thing and, in his very limited, hundred words of self-taught English, he could answer any question I asked. He knew the price of a water buffalo or a water melon. He walked through his village wearing his ground length cotton *galabaya* (long flowing caftan; traditional garment of men) with his head secured in a white cotton turban. The children ran out to greet him and he laid his hand gently on every little uncombed head and he greeted each child by name.

He had decided that he wanted to work with tourists and that his hundred or so words of English would be sufficient. I guess he was right—it worked with me and my two travel pals during that first visit. On the day of our meeting, he invited us to his village home to meet his family, and then invited us to accompany him and his wife and children to a *mulid* in the desert, a fair distance from his home. A *mulid* celebrates the birthday or saint's day of a deceased local holy man and some celebrations are very elaborate. Most have all the attributes of a carnival, complete with rides and games. This *mulid* was carnival-like, with the same type of rides we in the west are accustomed to, except that out in the middle of the *sahara* (desert) there is no electricity so the rides are operated by hand. It was a new experience, riding in a Ferris wheel that was started, turned, and stopped by a young man using his hands and often calling upon passersby for help. If he became distracted and didn't let go in time, then the wheel picked him up and carried him full circle while he hung on for dear life, with children and adults cheering him on.

As we traveled to the *mulid* site I counted thirty people in the back end of the canopied pick-up truck in which we were riding, many seated on the wooden benches that line the sides—a space that comfortably carries about twelve persons. It hastily transported us over the bumpy and rocky desert, leaving a giant cloud of sand-filled dust behind. Because there were no seats for them, the little children sat on our laps or crouched on the floor, under the legs of the adult women. Adult men hung on for dear life while riding on the outside rear and side bumpers, *their galabayas* puffed full with wind and giving the appearance of man-sized balloons attached to the outside of the pick-up truck.

If I mentioned that I was interested in fossils, the very next day we might climb to the top of the desert mountain over the Valley of the Kings and gather marine fossils, millions upon millions of years old, lying there since the high desert was on the bottom of the sea. Or we might gather prehistoric hand tools shaped from stone by stone.

He was an excellent horseman, and he rode a camel and a donkey with equal ease. We often rode together through the lush green fields enjoying the view from the lofty perch of a camel's back, swaying to and fro in rhythm. Or on horseback we might race along the sandy shores of the Nile. The many hours he had spent in the coffee houses playing dominos and backgammon had produced a mind quick with numbers. He lived just one village away from his birthplace. I doubt there was anything about this region Sayeed did not know, yet he had never attended school so he did not know how to read and write his own language and this embarrassed him not at all.

Sayeed was the husband of Jamalat. I spent a lot of time in their home over the twenty-plus years of going back and forth between America and Egypt. I was without family in Egypt and they wanted me to feel I was one of their family. There was a special closeness. We just cliqued.

On that first meeting, during my first trip to Egypt, I knew one word of Arabic: *shokran*. Jamalat, Sayeed's wife, knew one word of English: thank you. Already we could communicate verbally. We spoke the same word.

I liked Jamalat immediately. She was young and she radiated friendliness. Her dark eyes danced and her smile was warm, despite all the missing teeth. She carried herself well. I had a good feeling when I was with her. I have often maintained that women have a universal understanding and bonding. I've experienced it many times in my travels abroad. The thing that bonds us together is the knowledge that we each care most about the same things: our home and our family. Their simple one-room mud brick house, with a dirt floor so hard packed it made no dust when swept, was clean and well cared for. It showed pride.

Jamalat was the first of my Egyptian women friends to share all her family with me. It seems that we were always going to visit one of her sisters or her mother or grandmother. They were all just as warm and welcoming to me as Jamalat herself was. Most of her family lived in the west bank village of Gurna. But some of them lived further away, so this was my introduction to family life in the various small villages on the west side of the River Nile at Luxor.

I cared about their two young children, Hanem and Khalil, ages two and three years at the time. Sayeed and Jamalat taught their children to address me as "Mama Jonna," a name that continues today. Now, the children of those children address me as *Jidda* (Grandma).

Sayeed wasn't sure of his exact age, but I guessed him to be about twenty to twenty-five years younger than I. Yet the relationship we established reversed our ages and he became a father figure to me. At first I thought it was because he was so well established in that culture and I was a real novice. Even though he was shorter than I, figuratively speaking, I looked up to him as he was wiser and more knowledgeable than I about most of the things we dealt with on a daily basis.

Many years before making my first trip to Egypt I had a vision of myself lying on the ground in an Egyptian village, dead at age nineteen—murdered. My father stood over me, his face so contorted with grief that I could not recognize him. My father's identity seemed unimportant during the next few years—I was much more concerned with myself and why I was murdered and by whom. Finally, I just pushed it all aside in my mind, but I never forgot. When with Sayeed, little things happened often that I labeled déjà vu, such as certain familiar body language or a facial expression. Even a sneeze once made me think I had heard that exact sound previously. One day, while deep in my own meditation, I again saw myself lying dead in the village lane, with my grieving father standing over me. Yes, Sayeed definitely was the one standing there grief-stricken.

After much contemplation I decided to not mention any of this to Sayeed. My limited Arabic vocabulary and his limited use of English presented somewhat of a potential problem for such a delicate subject. I feared he may not understand and if he decided to label me as *magnuna* (crazy) I may have lost my close association with him and his family. I decided it just wasn't necessary to disclose this in order for our relationship to continue to grow. I very much regret that decision—it was probably a risk worth taking. It could have brought us even closer. I am sad that I doubted myself in that way! Deep down in my heart I think he knew.

When Jamalat became pregnant for the third time, Sayeed told me in his improving English, "If this child is woman child we name Jonna." Well, this baby was a woman child and now there are two of us Jonnas on the west bank of Luxor.

Sayeed ran into a major problem when he tried to register Jonna's birth and get a birth certificate for her. The authorities would not let him give her that name because it is not an Islamic name. They argued that she must have an Islamic name, even after he told them in Arabic, "I must have a daughter named Jonna. This is the name that is in my heart and this is the name she must have." Finally, in his frustration, Sayeed threw his hands into the air and said, "Give her any name you want." I learned just recently—sixteen years later—that Jonna's Islamic and official name on her birth certificate is *Warda* or Rose. But everyone knows her as Jonna.

Today I am very close to Jonna and I love to be with her. In a somewhat remote sense, we are like sisters. She likes to take me to school with her and I've spent many hours sitting in the classrooms with her and her friends.

It is through Jamalat that I began learning to cook Egyptian food. In her house there was not enough money to buy a cook stove, but she did have a little butane gas-operated single burner. Of course, there was no table, counter top, cabinet, chair or sink. Her single burner was outdoors in the mud-walled courtyard because there was no room that could be used as a kitchen. It sat on the bare ground and we squatted beside it to do the cooking. Her water was carried on her head from the village well, about six houses away, in a very heavy clay jar. The village well was the women's community meeting place, so it was doubly important to visit there every day.

One thing that was desperately needed in the house was a toilet. When nature's call came, family members trekked to the sugar cane fields, and there amongst the thick growth of the strong green stalks, they sought out the needed privacy. This did not protect them from the many rats, snakes, and scorpions that thrived in the sugar fields.

One year I gifted the family with the installation of a crude but adequate hole-in-the-ground squat toilet. This was built in the family courtyard. The toilet itself was surrounded with a chest high mud brick wall, providing privacy on all sides. But there was no roof because there was no rain in the desert and privacy above the chest wasn't an issue. It wasn't necessary, so it wasn't added. The danger of leakage means there can be no pipes for running water in or near a mud brick dwelling, so this could not be a flush operation—it was typical and common in this region. The user simply squats over the dry porcelain bowl which surrounds the hole in the ground. Toilet paper is not used. Using a container of water previously carried from the village well, the toilet user washes him or herself clean and then pours the remaining water down the toilet—thus, flushing it. This type of toilet is a very efficient operation, still in use today inside many homes throughout Egypt, and it was a thousand times better than going to the sugar cane fields.

In 2009 it was discovered that Sayeed suffered from a liver ailment and it was necessary for him to travel a long distance by train to a city in Middle Egypt to receive specialized medical attention. He was a very sick man and his wife and brothers accompanied him on the long uncomfortable journey. When surgery was called for, the family was perplexed. No one in this poor family had money for such a thing. I am very blessed that I was with the family at the time and that I had an opportunity and the means to make it possible for Sayeed to have the needed surgery. We treasured his company for many more months but we could see he was not showing signs of improvement. Walking was painful for him and his withering face showed signs of sadness. It was obvious that he wanted to be with his loved ones during every waking moment and we wanted to be with him as much as possible. Sadly, our beloved *Baba* (Papa) Sayeed departed from us recently. I was not in

11

Egypt when he made his transition, but I am filled with love and grief and Sayeed will live forever in my heart and memory. I am grateful for this family's twenty-two year presence in my life. Good bye for now, Baba.

Tea, Coffee House, Water Pipe

The national drink here in Egypt is steaming hot tea, served in small juice size glasses (no handles) with more sugar than anyone can imagine.

No matter how hot the weather or the time of day, *shy* (hot tea) is always in order. Most *shy* is in powder form and is made individually in each glass, almost like an instant drink, but it is not instant. I've never seen a tea bag in an Egyptian home.

Tea is automatically served if one is a guest. Tea is served in many shops for sipping while shopping. Trains have a man continuously going car to car selling hot tea. Long distance busses make stops for tea. While lounging on the beaches of the Red Sea and Mediterranean Sea resorts in the briefest of garments, a man or boy comes around selling hot tea. If I hire laborers for work around the house, it is my responsibility to serve them hot tea at regular intervals. I serve hot *shy* to my gardener. Men walk the streets of the major cities selling the freshly made brew. In the cities, tea boys run back and forth on the streets delivering glasses of the boiling hot drink to business men who are too busy to go outside. It is not possible to conduct business without a glass of *shy*. In Egypt I have never seen tea served in a plastic, paper or styrofoam cup.

A glass of freshly brewed hot tea cannot be picked up or held by my naked fingers. However, all Egyptians have no problem holding this glass of boiling brew. I guess many years of experience numbs ones fingers enough to make this possible and easy. Men also pick up white hot charcoal for their shisha and women lift lids from long simmering pots, all with bare fingers.

In this small glass of steaming hot tea, most Egyptians use between three to five heaping teaspoons of sugar. They do like it sweet! I join the group that likes to add some fresh or dried mint (called *na-na*) to the tea. A friend grows mint in her garden and generously gifts me with the fresh greenery, as she knows I like *shy bi na-na* (tea with mint).

Tea does not grow here in Egypt. Most of the tea that I drink is strong and a little harsh, probably not top quality. But that is the tea I have learned to love. Even in the harsh heat of summer, Egyptians never drink tea with ice.

A special occasion drink made in some coffee houses is freshly brewed karkaday, a tasty beverage made from dried red hibiscus blossoms. This delicious drink is enjoyed hot or cold and is often served as a welcome drink at major hotels. The best hibiscus flowers come from special fields near Aswan.

The Ghawah

Egypt is well known for the *ghawah* (coffee house), where coffee is rarely served, but hundreds of glasses of steaming hot tea are consumed each day and long into the night. Always at the *ghawah*, there are rickety chairs for sitting, a very small table for tea and games and *shisha* (water pipes). These are the necessities. A building or roof overhead is not a necessity and many *ghawah* don't have such.

Here in Upper Egypt, a *ghawah* can be set up alongside the road or street, or it may be under a shade tree or along the river bank, or even in a vacant lot. The setting is not important, but what is important is that it is a place for the men to relax, smoke a *shisha*, enjoy a game of *tawala* (backgammon) or dominos, watch the people and traffic going by, catch up on the news and gossip, visit with old friends while making new friends, conduct business, and nowadays, maybe watch a favorite television program or soccer match. This is where secrets are told and tales are spread. It serves as the social center of the neighborhood.

This is not a place for Egyptian women—at least not here in Upper Egypt. However, in Cairo and other metropolitan areas, I notice that women are welcome and they do congregate together at the coffee houses.

In the cities the *ghawah* has more style and personality than in Upper Egypt. Even in Luxor, just now three new stylish coffee houses have opened. Mostly I see foreign women there, but the Egyptian women are starting to come.

Amongst friends, it seems that anything goes at the ghawah. I was having tea with longtime friend, Zacharia, when one of his buddies came in and requested that Zach give him an injection. The friend had been to the doctor, who sent him to the pharmacy to buy the injection. He was to find someone to inject him with the medicine—or he could inject himself. The two men stepped behind a skinny column, the friend lifted his *galabaya* to reveal his upper thigh, and Zach, with no expertise, injected the medicine into him. Tea and *shisha* continued as usual.

Shisha

*S*hisha is the Egyptian word for the water pipe, famous all over the Middle East, but called by different names, *hookah* or *nargilah* to name a couple. Calling it a hubbly bubbly will label one instantly as an uninformed tourist and is not the best way to win Egyptian friends. *Shisha* is very serious business. A *ghawah* is usually necessary for smoking the shisha. It is probably safe to say that more *shisha* is served in the *ghawah* than *shy*.

Many homes have a *shisha* and it is often smoked at home. In the privacy of home, some women even enjoy a *shisha*. In major cities, where nicer facilities for tea and *shisha* thrive, it is not uncommon to see sophisticated women enjoying this activity in public.

In Egypt, the common term is *shrib shisha* (drink *shisha*), rather than smoking shisha. All my inquiries as to why it is called drinking, rather than smoking, have met a dead end. But from those conversations I have drawn my own conclusion that it comes from the act of inhaling, therefore, swallowing or drinking.

A special tobacco is used and it is placed wet into the small clay bowl at the top of the pipe, often covered with foil punched full of holes to let the fire through, then the white hot burning charcoal tops it off. As the smoker draws on the mouth piece, the hot air is drawn down the narrow glass neck, from the tobacco, and is passed through the water for cooling, then back up and into the mouth (and lungs!) of the smoker.

Outside of this culture, this tobacco is sometimes confused with hashish or other drugs. There will always be those who choose to use the water pipe this way, but it is rare and illegal drugs will never be seen at the coffee house. The men sitting in the *gahwah* are smoking very fine tobacco, often heavily flavored with fruit and containing no chemicals, they stress.

It brings me much pleasure to watch the sunset from our garden terrace while looking across the desert to Howard Carter's* house and the King's Valley, with my *shisha* in hand. My favorite tobacco is flavored with *tofah* (apple or apple with molasses). When we have guests in our home, we fire up the shisha for a little social smoking.

It is sad to say that very few Egyptians have good looking teeth. Most teeth bear the stains of a lifetime of too much tea and too much shisha and cigarettes and no dental care.

---

* Howard Carter is the British archaeologist who discovered King Tut's tomb

Marriage Proposal

I had been settled into my first Luxor apartment just a few weeks in 1995 when Karima, my neighbor on the floor above mine, stepped outside her door and called down the unpainted cement stairwell, with two broken steps, to say there was a phone call for me. I had no phone and I wondered who might know that I could be contacted through Karima.

She had a scarf tossed lightly over her head. If any male entered the stairwell, she could quickly secure her *hijab* (head scarf) and have every hair properly covered. However, if she did happen to meet a male in the stairwell, if he were well mannered and followed the teachings of the Quran he would cast his eyes downward and politely speak without looking at her (Quran 24:30,31). I ran quickly up the stairs, jumping over the broken steps, without stopping to cover my hair. Wearing the veil was not a life-long habit for me and it was easy to forget. "It's a man," she whispered. I wondered why the whispering; we were alone. Her children were in school and her husband was at work. I didn't realize at the time how unusual it was for a single woman to speak with a man.

"My name is Salama. I'm a friend of Abdel Aliem," he said in flawless English. How thrilled I was to hear his association with Abdel Aliem, my Egyptian friend and former teacher in the U.S. I had temporarily lost contact with him and I was very happy that someone was about to bring me news from him. I knew his family in America and they were planning a move back to Egypt when we last spoke. Salama and I exchanged traditional morning greetings in English. Before I could ask about my dear *lost* friend, the caller continued, "Abdel Aliem tells me you love Egypt very much."

"Yes I do. When did Abdel Aliem and Madame arrive in Egypt?" I wanted news, but it was as if I had not asked the question.

"Would you ever consider marrying and staying in Egypt?" he inquired.

Odd question, I thought. "Well, of course I'd consider it under the appropriate circumstances. Is Abdel Aliem's house finished and are the children adjusting?" I tried again.

"Well that's why I'm calling." Again, he ignored my questions. "I'm looking for a wife and Abdel Aliem said you are very intelligent, we are about the same age, and he says you would be a good wife. I am divorced from my first wife and my children are married. I have no other wives. I own a villa in Sadaat City and a large farm and villa in the delta, right along the Nile. I have a doctorate degree from the university. I drive a Mercedes. Under the Quran I can marry a Christian. I would not require you to become Muslim. Are you interested in marrying me?"

I have survived being caught off-guard in a number of situations but I was not prepared for this question. Never had I received a serious and sincere marriage proposal by telephone from a man I had never met, seen or talked with. I opened my mouth to speak but the sound did not come. Why hadn't he given me some warning that he was going to offer marriage?

I was aware that in Egypt there was no courtship as I know it in the west—no getting to know each other before marriage. I knew that being in love was not a component to be considered. Still I had never applied these thoughts and criteria to myself.

It seemed like an endless amount of time before I managed to find my tongue. I breathed a prayer that I would think of something appropriate to say. I didn't want to stumble as I searched for the words. I wanted to be kind and polite. I said something to the effect that I am sure he would be an excellent husband, but that I am not thinking about marriage at this time. I'm sure my voice rose to a higher pitch. I thanked him for his consideration. I wondered what an Egyptian woman would do in this situation. Well, actually I know what she would do: she would jump at the chance and say "yes." He was a good catch.

I bade him an awkward farewell. Then I breathed a prayer of thanks that I did not have to say all that in Arabic.

Karima is an English teacher and she heard and understood everything on my end of the conversation. She was wide-eyed. Women are the same all over the world: she wanted to hear every little detail. Karima dashed into her kitchen to quickly prepare two glasses of steaming sweet tea and we sat down for girl talk. Words flow so much more easily over a glass of hot tea.

I relayed the details to Karima, including the list of Salama's credentials. Karima was very thoughtful and serious. Finally, she spoke. "Madame Jonna, I think you should not have refused his offer of marriage. I think this man is a good man. You should have asked your friend Abdel Aliem about him. This man owns two villas and a farm in the delta. He drives a Mercedes. He is a rich man and you could have a good life."

No mention of love or affection. No mention of personalities, habits, interests, or any of the other things that a western woman takes into account when considering marriage. Marriage in Egypt is business.

A good man/woman and *a good life* are what I heard over and over when references were made to engagement or marriage. This is what everyone is in search of. Yet, I never figured out just what constitutes a *good man* or *good woman*. The only thing more important is that the prospective spouse comes from a *good family*. That is easier to understand. Without the *good family* there can be no talk of engagement, no matter how *good* the man or woman is and no matter what *a good life* is promised.

When I asked about love, the answer was always the same: "Love comes after marriage." When I asked a new bride or groom the same question, the answer was always casual, "Oh yes, I love him," or more often, "No I don't love him yet, but I will love him." Indeed I did meet some lucky couples who were very much in love, both before marriage and after many years of matrimony.

Early the next morning, Karima again called down the cement stairwell, announcing that I had a phone call. Surely he was not calling again. "*Sabah el Khir* (good morning), Madame Jonna." It was great to hear the voice of my friend, Abdel Aliem. We exchanged all the typical morning greetings in both Arabic and English, and then we inquired about the health, family and travel of each other.

I could speak English or Arabic with Abdel Aliem. For two years in America, he had been my weekly private tutor for Arabic and he was my teacher of the Holy Quran. All that aside, I knew the real reason for this telephone call, but no Egyptian would ever open a conversation without the common formalities, inquiries, and the proper acknowledgements to God.

"I think you made a mistake to refuse Salama. He is a good man and he is rich. He has two villas and a farm and a Mercedes. He knows important people. I think you should change your mind and come here to our city and meet him. I can arrange the meeting and be with you," Abdel Aliem offered.

Partly out of curiosity, and partly out of respect for Abdel Aliem, I agreed to a meeting. "But, I do not want to meet him in Sadaat City" I said. "I want to meet only the man, away from his environment. I do not want to be influenced by his wealth or his surroundings. I invite you to bring Dr. Salama here to Luxor." Abdel Aliem was impressed with my statement and I knew I had said the right thing. He gave praises to God and the meeting was quickly arranged.

At Salama's request I made a reservation for him at "the finest hotel in Luxor" and agreed to meet him shortly after his flight from Cairo arrived. He was traveling alone and was waiting in the lobby of the famous five-star Winter Palace Hotel when I arrived. My tailored grey skirt was ankle length and my silk-looking polyester blouse was neatly tucked into the waist band and closed high on my neck. Over my hair I wore a bright colored silk scarf, folded and secured under my chin, in the fashion of Upper Egypt and Luxor. It was tight around my face and cascaded very properly downward, hiding my bosom. My make-up was conservative. Indeed, I looked like a *good* woman.

I had no particular feelings. I wasn't nervous. I wasn't excited. I wasn't looking forward to this meeting and I wasn't *not* looking forward to it. Actually, I felt rather "official," much as if I were going to a job interview.

Salama was tall and pleasant looking—not what I would call handsome. He was nicely dressed in casual western apparel that indicated quality and wealth. Actually, his face looked a bit like former President Sadaat. I wish I could say that Salama was charming and delightful. He was proper, educated and enjoyable in conversation. He did not flirt and neither did I. There was no trying to impress the other, no cute remarks or come-ons. For two days he stayed in Luxor and we lunched and dined and drank tea in the town's nicest places. Being a proper Muslim, he excused himself at prayer time and he used no alcohol.

We had very nice conversations. I realized that I could talk with him about some things that no one I knew in Luxor had ever heard of, like artists Picasso and Monet; like musicians Beethoven and Brahms. He was well traveled and knew the location of Argentina and Norway.

In the same matter-of-fact way Salama had presented his credentials, he continued to inform me of his expectations. If I agreed to marry him, we would marry the next day and I would leave Luxor with him immediately. I protested, "If I just disappear tomorrow, all my friends will have the police looking for me. No one knows about you and I need time to explain myself and to say farewell to many people here." Then Salama told me he would buy me a white gold wedding ring, because white gold is better. Had he asked, I would have let him know how much I love the beautiful richness of the twenty-one karat gold jewelry worn by the Egyptian women, and sold by the gram in the local gold bazaars.

Salama said we would spend our honeymoon in Malaysia because he had never traveled there. Actually, neither had I, so that may have been alright. Next, I was informed that I could not be away from him more than five nights during the course of a year. Whoa!!! How will I visit my family in America and take care of business there, I wondered.

Now it was time to really get serious. Without embarrassment, and in his same matter-of-fact style, Salama told me how *much* sex he expected, and in detail, *what* he expected and which positions he favored. This time, he *did* ask my opinion, but I couldn't tell him it all sounded very pre-planned, textbook-like and terribly boring. Apparently, there was no place in his bedroom for spontaneity or creativity or even passion—just routine.

He seemed generous. As soon as we reached Cairo, he would buy me a complete new wardrobe, Salama said. I wondered if I would have the privilege of making any choices for myself. He also offered to support my unmarried daughter in America and suggested that she should move to Egypt and live with us. Here unmarried women and men always remain in the family home until their marriage.

It was now deadline time. He wanted an answer. After all, it had been two days. This was not a decision that I dwelled upon. This was business and I treated it as such. My answer came easily. He merely responded, "I wish your answer were different. I will check to see if I can get an earlier flight to Cairo. You are welcome in my home at any time and I will always treat you with respect.

Wouldn't it be wonderful if all ending *courtships* closed so amicably? I never saw or spoke with Salama again. About three weeks later I heard he had a wife.

Learning the Arabic Language

After my third or fourth visit to Egypt, I began to realize how much I was missing because I couldn't speak Arabic. Most of the men I knew spoke a little English because they worked with tourists. I was spending more time with the women and children and I felt handicapped because I couldn't converse properly with them. There was only one remedy for that: learn to speak Arabic.

As simple as that I would learn to speak Arabic while I was at home in America. Was I in for a surprise! In the USA in the early nineties one didn't just enroll at the university or the local adult education program for a course in Egyptian Arabic. Few people were interested in learning Arabic. To complicate matters, I only wanted to learn the language of Egypt, which is different in dialect from the Arabic spoken in Morocco or Syria or Lebanon. Often it's difficult even for native speakers to understand the other's dialect.

Most Egyptians can't completely understand the Arabic of Saudi Arabia, for example, but most Saudis understand the Arabic of Egypt—and there's good reason for that. Egypt is the largest producer of movies, literature, poetry, pop music, and television shows. They are distributed all over the Arabic speaking world. Where in Colorado could I learn Egyptian Arabic?

Timidly, I telephoned the local mosque and explained the situation, inquiring if there might be an Egyptian who would like to teach me. The emam with whom I spoke said he would post a notice on the bulletin board. In just two days I received a response from an Egyptian man who identified himself as Abdel Aliem. We met. We negotiated financial terms, and the lessons began. For two years we met weekly in my home while I studied and he tutored.

No language is easy to learn when it uses a different alphabet and a different form of writing. The most difficult part of this learning experience was that I had no one to practice with or no opportunity to hear the language spoken. At that point I was satisfied to learn to speak only. The elegant script of the written language would wait.

Several years later when visiting Morocco, an Arabic speaking country, I was trying to use my language ability as much as possible. Before I could finish even the first sentence, the listener routinely exclaimed, "Oh, you are Egyptian!" Well, I don't think for one minute that I appeared as such but it was very obvious that I communicate in a language spoken in Egypt. Even within this country, there is a difference in the sound of the language from north to south and from east to west.

I know people who studied this language for two or more years at the university level, who can read and write Arabic well, but when visiting an Arabic speaking country they cannot speak or understand the spoken language. That is because the spoken and the written languages are different. The standard or formal, or modern, or classic language is the proper and written language. The colloquial, or the street language, is the spoken one and it isn't written. In Egypt the estimate is that just over sixty-four percent of the people are illiterate, therefore the speech may not be as refined as the written word. I cannot read or write this language, but I communicate verbally using the street language and I've never had an issue trying to make myself understood.

Those who are unfamiliar with Arabic often think two or more Egyptians talking together are arguing or fighting. That's not the situation at all. The language just calls for raised voices for emphasis.

Even though it's a very loud language, I like it. The language is very closely tied to the religion and hardly a sentence can be said or a response given without invoking God. The response to "how are you?" might be a very simple "thanks be to God," implying that no matter if one is doing well or feeling absolutely rotten, there is still much reason to thank God.

My favorite response might be *inshAllah* (if God wills it.) When I'm asked a question or a request is made of me and I want to be noncommittal, "*inshAllah*" is the perfect response. This is also said anytime a reference to the future is made, whether it is a reference to the next micro-second or to the next ten years. The message here is that God is totally in charge of our lives and nothing happens without His willing it to happen.

Arabic is the language of the Quran and this holy book cannot be translated or transliterated into any other language. My own Quran is printed in Arabic with English explanations telling me what each verse says—but this is not a translation.

I've seen this language labeled as one of the most difficult languages to learn, probably because the alphabet is different, therefore the script is different and it is written and read from the right side of the page to the left side. Therefore, books are read from what we would call the *back* to the *front* of the book.

Arabic has sounds that are not in the English language, and creating these sounds is difficult to nearly impossible for an English speaker. The particular throat muscles we need for these sounds have never been exercised or developed. When I began to speak the sounds of Arabic, I had a very bad sore throat for weeks as I exercised those particular muscles, the same as exercising any unused muscles.

Arabic speakers learning English have the same problems. In their language there is no sound for the letter "P" therefore this sound is nearly impossible to make and it comes out with the sound of "B". Children call their father "papa," as in English, but it has the sound of "*baba*." The *airport* is the *airbort*. *Passport* becomes *bassbort*. Recently I purchased a booklet of papyrus note pads, identified in writing on the cover as a "Writing Bad." It is a lovely language and I enjoy using it. I wish we could adopt some Arabic features into our own language.

A number of years ago when I was just learning Arabic, a Cairo shopkeeper invited me to enjoy a cup of tea while I shopped. This is very common and acceptable in Egypt, where the customer sits in a comfortable chair or sofa and sips the tea while the staff brings the goods to him or her for inspection. As we drank our tea and conversed, his youthful helper found much humor in our antics. We probably sounded like three year old children, as I was struggling in the most basic Arabic and the shopkeeper was having the same difficulty in the most beginner English. Laughing, the helper wanted to know why we didn't speak our own languages. It would be so much easier. That made more sense to him. The answer was simple: had I spoken English at my normal rate of speech and used my typical vocabulary, he could not have understood me, nor could I have understood him if he did the same. As it was, we chatted for a good length of time and though ultra-basic and in two different languages, we had a delightful conversation.

Learning About the Religion

I was delighted to learn that Abdel Aliem was a lifelong student and teacher of the Holy Quran. Since he was teaching me to speak Arabic, I asked him to be my religion teacher also. I did not intend to convert to Islam, but I wanted to know everything about it. I knew I could never understand the culture of Egypt if I didn't understand the religion that created that culture. That was the best decision I made!

A college educated man, Abdel Aliem had lived in the USA for a good part of his adult life. He and his Egyptian wife have four children, all born in America. He is a very pious Muslim who does not believe in touching a woman who is outside his immediate family. Other than an introductory handshake—when he politely bent to my tradition—during the two years we met weekly we never had any physical contact—not even an accidental brush of the fingertips when exchanging a paper. I respect him greatly.

I often thought he enjoyed the challenge of teaching me. The language portions of our sessions were rather mundane, but the religion portion sometimes became a little challenging. I never intended to be antagonistic, but I had to question many things in order to understand them.

He was very patient. Some of what I learned I never understood. Sometimes I merely accepted what was written and explained, hoping that understanding might come later. We often had lengthy philosophical discussions which were interesting and enlightening, due to the differences in eastern and western thinking. I was learning his way and he was learning mine.

I was not the only one learning something new. I seriously doubt that he had ever been challenged by a female or had debated with a woman before our paths crossed and I am sure he has not had that honor since.

I am so grateful that I took the time to pursue this avenue of learning. It helped tremendously in my acceptance of the Egyptian people and in their feelings toward me. It made no difference to my Egyptian friends that I was not Islamic. In fact, the subject rarely came up. Since many Egyptians are illiterate they have never read the Quran for themselves and sometimes their knowledge and understanding are less than correct. Many times they came to me to settle a disagreement, or simply to inquire about what the Quran says. They sensed my respect for them and their religion and they trusted that I would be truthful with them.

While I did not embrace Islam, I came to love and treasure many aspects of it and have adopted some things for myself. When I'm away from Egypt I miss the five times daily prayer call, the morning prayers which open the state-run radio and television stations, and the prayer from the cabin speakers before an EgyptAir flight. I miss certain phrases in the language, so laced with acknowledgements to God.

Deir El Bahari:
The Opera Aida

S itting in the middle of the *sahara (desert)*, far from any city, under a deep rosy-yellow full moon, I was watching a professional performance of Verdi's opera, complete with symphony orchestra from Cairo. I had to pinch myself to be sure this was all real. The opera Aida was staged right here on the ground in front of the beautiful Mortuary Temple of Queen Hatshepsut, also identified as Dier el Bahari, all on the *west* bank of the *sahara* at Luxor. Here people live in mud houses and commonly sleep on their rooftops during the hot nights of summer. This night they would fall asleep to opera music.

Queen Hatshepsut, who declared herself Pharaoh Hatshepsut, was one of Egypt's few female rulers and definitely the best known. She dressed as a typical pharaoh, even donning the false beard, a symbol of pharaoh's strength. The most unusual, beautiful, and architecturally different mortuary temple in the land was built for this female ruler, and her architect, Senamut, is honored with a burial tomb in front of her temple—a rarity to say the least. However, he was never buried there and his place of burial has never been found. Rumors have persisted for three thousand five hundred years that the Queen and Senamut were lovers, probably because he (a commoner) is shown carved into her temple wall affectionately holding one of her children. Then there is the ancient graffiti on the wall of a grotto, high in the cliffs above her temple. The drawings are crude but the actions portrayed leave no question as to why this is called "the dirty grotto" and no question that the two persons in the drawing are the Queen and Senemut. There is no proof to support this speculation.

I know for certain: this is the only temple from ancient Egypt that I visit every time I return to this country. It pulls me back. The temple is elegant and sophisticated; the perfect setting for a queen and for an opera. This opera's two hour story takes place in Egypt. The first performance was in Cairo in 1871. In 1997 in Egypt, this performance was a major international event with dignitaries, royalty, heads of countries and jet setters in attendance. Of course, they usually attend on opening night when the lowest price ticket on the far back rows is three hundred US dollars. I attended the last night and paid fifty dollars for my near-the-front seat and another twenty dollars for transportation.

The five-star Winter Palace Hotel on the *east* side arranged the transportation for all of us ticket-holding tourists. We were as fancily dressed as any tourist could be. Most of us did not travel with an opera-going wardrobe. I think I got a slight idea of how it feels to be a celebrity. Our large luxurious air conditioned coach the hotel arranged for us had a spiffily dressed handsome young, white-gloved policeman, imported from Cairo. Outside, we also merited police escorts on motorcycles with swirling red lights to stop all traffic for us. The route was lined with white uniformed policemen, standing at attention until the time came to salute as we sped by.

There were no bridges crossing the river near Luxor and thus, no efficient way to transport all these opera-goers back and forth across the River Nile every evening for seven days. They could not be expected to ride the rather crude public ferry, with the worn and splintered wooden seats. Egypt's military came to the rescue and laid a floating bridge. This was the same type of bridge they spread across the Suez Canal in 1973 during the Ramadan/Yom Kipper war with Israel. The bridge looked like heavy rectangular boards hinged together on the edges, but flexible enough to ride the waves and withstand the swift current of the Nile—and still support these large, heavy coaches driving on top of them. But this particular floating bridge was special and unlike a piece of military equipment, it was also covered with six hundred meters of red carpet adorned with gold lotus flowers. Approaching from the east, the bridge looked like a very small red ribbon stretching a half mile across the Nile, bobbing up and down, swaying and rippling with the current.

As exciting as it was, to be riding on a large luxury coach crossing the River Nile on a floating bridge was more than a little disconcerting. With my face pressed flat against the window, I could not see the bridge under our tires so I had the unsettling feeling that we were driving right on top of the water, at a point where the Nile runs deep and swift.

Still leading our small parade of three plush coaches—and sharing our floating bridge—were all the policemen on motorcycles with red lights flashing. For all those watching from the safety of the river banks it must have been a spectacular sight. I kept wondering if the bridge could hold us all. It felt as if I was experiencing some part of a miracle. Of course, we were not walking on water, but how much closer to *that* event could we be? Would we need another miracle when we returned to Luxor on this bridge after dark?

The opera's performance area appeared to be about half the size of a football field and the only scenery in the background was Queen Hatshepsut's magnificent temple, glowing from inside with colored lights as it nestled against the surrounding towering limestone cliffs. The cast numbered into the hundreds, as there were many non-singing soldiers in the opera, chosen from the youthful men of the nearby villages. They were clad in nothing but ancient style kilts and as the moon moved away from our area, their brown bodies continued to glisten. As the orchestra, imported from Cairo, began tuning up, the cascade of notes resounded melodiously throughout the entire desert valley.

After all the excitement and emotion of our coach ride, and now the music swelling in the night, a certain peace enveloped me and I settled comfortably into my seat, sat back and enjoyed the performance.

Instantly I was caught up in Verdi's tragic tale of jealousy, power, politics, war, treason and, of course, forbidden love between the captain of the Egyptian guard, Radamis, and one of his captives, the exquisite Aida. She was not a typical captive. The daughter of the King of Ethiopia, Aida was captured during warfare in her native country at a time when all captives were marched back to Egypt and made to serve as slaves. Upon learning of the love and passion between Aida and his army chief, Radamis, Pharaoh lost trust and confidence in his favored officer and sentenced him to languish in a prison cell until death ended his suffering. Aida chose to secretly hide in the cell and die with her lover.

The tragic ending of the opera left most of us in a pensive mood and there was little chatter or laughter as we left our seats and headed toward our coach. Or maybe there was little gayety because opera-goers were thinking of the after-dark return trip to Luxor.

I could not see anything as I looked down from inside the coach—just black water with a small hint of moonlight glistening on it periodically. I quickly realized that if my anxiety continued to mount, I'd be a basket case before we reached the other side. Fortunately, my years of meditation practice took charge of my thinking and calmed my anxious mind. I was the only person on the coach who appeared to reach Luxor in a calm and reasonably relaxed state.

Not long after this evening a very long bridge was completed about ten miles south of Luxor, making it possible to cross the Nile via automobile. My night in the desert at the opera was the last time the floating bridge was used in Upper Egypt. It was also the last time, to date, that Aida was performed in the Luxor region.

I recorded this October 19, 1997.

The Massacre

The west bank Mortuary Temple of Queen Hatshepsut, also
known as Deir el Bahari is at the top of the *must see* list for all
tourists to the region. For almost four thousand years it has stood there
beckoning, framed by a half circle of extremely high sheer limestone
cliffs, welcoming all who wish to come and enjoy its unique architecture
and beauty.

This is a place where tourists never seem in a hurry to leave. The
magnificent wall carvings beg for attention because of the stories they
tell; stories about the Queen's life and her royal successes. Her twenty
year reign began as regent for her infant step-son, Thutmose III. She
then gave herself the title of pharaoh and served her country and her
people well. Tourists seem to enjoy being at the site. There's no urgency.
There's no time pressure. It's a *feel good* place.

No one at the temple on this very hot autumn day will remember it
in this manner. November 17, 1997 was the day of the horrific massacre
that brutally and barbarically killed 62 persons—58 of them tourists—at
Deir el Bahari. Total bedlam broke out as men, women and children ran
about madly screaming—consumed by fear and confusion—their eyes
darting about wildly. People were running about and dropping dead
all around them. They could hear the gunshots echoing through the
temple and even through the valley. Where could they go? What could
they do? Which direction were the shots coming from? Where were their

children? The crazy men with the big machetes were hacking people to death. They were cutting open their guts and spilling them out. Where's the tour guide who brought them here? A man trying to be helpful was yelling instructions in Arabic—but what was he saying? The death of many came after their mutilation and disembowelments. A few fortunate ones managed to run and hide, hopefully saving their own lives. It was a scene straight from a hell that few of us could ever imagine.

There was no warning or concern that anything like that could ever happen, so there was no major security at the site—or any other site. The temples have very peacefully and quietly stood there for thousands of years without a problem or incident. I've been told that it took the police over one hour to arrive after being called. The area of Luxor had never experienced anything like this and to say that citizens, peacekeepers and officials were totally unprepared would be a gross understatement. The town didn't even have an ambulance.

I had been in my Luxor flat most of the day, unaware of the events just a short distance from me. When I took a late afternoon outing I was very surprised to see the Egyptian men and women standing in the Luxor streets looking stunned and openly sobbing. They were devastated and they felt some responsibility because this event happened in their own country, in their own locale. They didn't want the world to think that Egyptians were murderers. It didn't take me long to share their state of grief and to join them in their extreme sorrow and tears.

Suddenly the place was inundated with police, flown in from Cairo. The entire west bank was placed under quarantine and curfew. Innocent citizens could not leave their homes. Children couldn't attend school. As might be expected, rumors and tall tales ran rampant. The Egyptian government withheld most information, as usual.

Friends and family in the U.S. learned this news from their televisions and understanding only the words "Luxor" and "Egypt" they panicked, thinking I could have been involved. They knew more about the events than I did. The telephone in my flat rang almost constantly for two days. I learned of the machete mutilation of most of the women's bodies, and heard about a note praising Islam being placed inside the disemboweled body of another victim. I learned that four of the murdered couples were honeymooning and that there were small children among those massacred.

It is generally believed that the six terrorists—four of whom committed suicide or were murdered by each other—were college students from southern Egypt and the unofficial talk on the street is that the operation was financed by Osama Bin Laden. It's been a long time, but Egypt says the investigation is on-going. Countries that lost citizens are still waiting for answers and compensation from Egypt.

Most of Egypt's economy is tourist based and at the hint of a negative situation, the tourists stop coming. More than 12.8 million tourists visit Egypt yearly, spending over U.S. $11.6 billion. A lack of tourists in the country presented untold hardship for one of Luxor's finest five-star hotels because it was necessary for the hotel to let their staff go. With no business prospects on the horizon, they were forced to close their doors. Public city transport had to stop simply because nobody could afford the eight cents it cost to ride.

Healing Ceremony
at Deir El Bahri

It had been two months since the horrific massacre and Luxor continued to be like a ghost town, rather than the thriving bustling tourist center it was before the violent event. There were no tourist ships cruising up and down the Nile. About one hundred were docked at Luxor and another one hundred were docked at Aswan. Hotels remained closed. The main topic of conversation was the massacre. Everyone continued to speculate about who was responsible for this horror. One good thing was that the new bridge crossing the Nile, ten miles south of Luxor, was finished and automobiles could now cross the river in either direction. The bridge opening was reason for a grand celebration, but because of the circumstances, the occasion was downplayed.

President Mubarak's government decided to sponsor a *healing* ceremony at the outdoor site of the massacre—the Mortuary Temple of Queen Hatshepsut at Deir el Bahari—and I was invited. Invitations were sent to all Egypt's elite and well-known people, such as actors, musicians, the wealthy or highly placed, known politicians, etc. The citizenry did not receive invitations but were permitted to witness the ceremony, from a standing area a lengthy distance behind all the seated dignitaries. The very heavily armed policemen—imported from Cairo—may have outnumbered the citizens.

For the invitees there were nice folding chairs placed on top of woven authentic Egyptian carpets, which were spread over a large area of desert. I felt like a celebrity myself, sitting in the *sahara* on a comfortable chair, starlight glistening overhead, carpets underfoot and listening to the Cairo Symphony Orchestra performing live—the second time for me to have that privilege in that setting.

I sat in the sixth row, where I could plainly see President Mubarak and Madame, award winning author Naguib Mahfouz, actor Omar Sharif and others I recognized from television—each just a few rows from me. I can get very lost in my thoughts listening to the orchestra play. I forget where I am—but this time I could not forget. The symphony orchestra sounds a hundred times more powerful when it performs in the desert, rather than in an enclosed concert hall. I remembered the beautiful, as well as the horrific events that had recently happened at this very place.

So how did I get invited to this elite event? I saw no other foreigners in the area where I sat—only celebrity types. There was a newcomer to Luxor, an Egyptian, and nobody knew anything about him. He seemed to not like to talk about himself and our questions were treated with vague and incomplete answers. He was from Cairo and occasionally his daughters came to visit him, but he had no friends or acquaintances in town and it appeared he wanted it that way. He seemed like a gentle and kind man and he befriended me, as we liked to eat at the same small restaurant. Then he said he liked for me to have tea with him after the meal so that he could practice his English, which was already quite good. This became almost a daily ritual.

It was whispered to me that this man is "a big man" and that means he is very important. My invitation came from him. I began to realize just how "big" this man might be as he drove to the ceremony site, with me in the back seat and his daughter in the front beside him.

Security was extremely tight and traffic was backed up for a mile, while police checked all autos and passengers. Roads were sealed off to regular traffic. Yet as we approached each check point, a policeman intercepted us and with a snappy salute, waved us around all vehicles and right through to the next checkpoint—all without a look in the car or a word exchanged. No one questioned the wide-eyed foreign woman sitting in the back seat, too bewildered to ask questions.

In the following weeks, as rumors made their rounds in Luxor, I learned that my host was the Chief of Police in Cairo and he had been involved in actions that created the need for him to get out of Cairo and go to Luxor (over 400 miles away) and live incognito for several months. His very life depended on no one knowing who or where he was. Cairo jails are not the safest places in the city and have often made news because of the violence against the prisoners. There were an unusually large number of inmate deaths in the Cairo jails that year due to official police torture and many of the deaths were especially horrific and brutal. This was making international news and was receiving a lot of attention in the world media and from international human rights groups. Of course, the police chief was ultimately responsible for these horrific murders and now his own life was at stake. I'm glad I was unaware of the chief's identity when I accepted his invitation. But I had a most enjoyable evening.

Meeting Omran

The last thing I expected that warm spring morning was to meet someone of interest. I tried to avoid Luxor as much as possible when I was staying at my favorite west bank hotel, The Amon. For me, staying at this seven-room family-run hotel for a few nights was the same as staying with friends or family. There's an atmosphere of calmness about the west side that just doesn't exist on the east side. If one arrives in Luxor via the public ferry boat, from the west side of the River Nile, one must pass through the brigade of boatmen, *felucca* men, carriage drivers and taxis, all vying for the tourist business. As much as I'm accustomed to the hassling from these men, I still can't help becoming annoyed at their non-stop persistence. Luxor has a reputation for being the hassle capital of Egypt.

On this lovely morning my agenda was to stroll around outside of the ancient Luxor Temple, with its one beautiful obelisk (the other half of the pair is at the Place de la Concorde in Paris), and survey all the new excavation now being done and to just be "in the moment" with myself and the project before me. I wanted a memory that I could take home with me, as I was planning to return to America in a matter of days.

A few years ago there was a small weedy public garden behind the temple, with unattractive apartment buildings and tacky shops surrounding it. This has been removed and an attractive two block long promenade has been installed in its place. It appears to be well-used by the local people and young families, and that had been my great concern. With the garden removed, I was concerned that the local Egyptians would have no place for their own relaxation and social time and fearful that Luxor would become a city designed for tourists only.

I had barely stepped onto the promenade when a handsome stranger with a head full of thick curly black hair, greeted me with a cheery English "good morning." I responded the same to him in Arabic, "*Sabah el khir.*" He froze in his tracks. He thought he had just smiled and spoken to a fellow Egyptian. An Egyptian man approaching an Egyptian woman would be extremely brazen and impolite and if he didn't immediately apologize and get out of there, he could be in big trouble.

This is also exactly how the best hustlers make their approach to tourists. I don't recall all the details of this street encounter, but I remember that contrary to previous encounters, it felt right and good to be talking to him and without hesitation I accepted his invitation for a glass of hot tea at the open-air coffee shop across the street.

We had so much to talk about—it was as if we would not have time to get it all said. We were like old friends getting together—though we were total strangers just ten minutes ago. I knew what he was going to say before he said it and he could finish my sentences for me. He showed no signs of trying to sell me anything or solicit anything from me and when he said "I feel like I've known you for a thousand years," I thought, yes *now* here comes his sales pitch and he's got me cornered here in this coffee shop. But not even a hint of sales pitch came my way. He was actually sincere in what he said. His English was good and he appeared very western in his faded blue jeans.

After we had drunk our tea and finished smoking our *shisha* (water pipe), we walked back to the promenade and on to Luxor Temple. Like any other tourist, we walked inside and surveyed the situation, taking photographs and discussing the various aspects of the temple. Afterward, as we walked along the promenade outside the temple, we were continuously stopped by the plain clothes tourist police who requested to see the papers of my new friend, Omran—papers allowing him to walk and talk with a tourist. Without those papers, such a man just might be hustling and forcing himself on the unsuspecting foreign woman.

I knew this routine and from past experiences, I knew well what my role should be. Yes, when the police stopped him and Omran had no papers for tourists, they threatened to take him to jail. I had known this man for an hour or two, but I stepped in and told them, in Arabic, that this is my husband. The language usage validated the "husband" claim. If he were a hustler and I had just met this man, then it's unlikely I would know how to speak Arabic. We went through this routine four times that morning so I knew then that he did not usually hang around this place or the police would know him.

From Luxor Temple we entered the mosque of Abu el Haggag, which was in the on-going process of repair and restoration. I had always been fascinated with this building, a portion of which was built in the twelfth century. However, most of the mosque we see today was built in the mid nineteenth century and continues to pay tribute to the beloved holy man, Abu el Haggag, who is called Luxor's patron saint.

In the nineteenth century as Egyptians and European adventurers looked for a place to build their dwellings, the abandoned four thousand year old Luxor Temple seemed ideal, right on the banks of the Nile and surrounded and protected by the high temple walls. So a village was built inside the temple. Of course, the village needed a mosque so the Abu el Hagagg site was added to and increased in size. Over the centuries dirt and sand accumulated in and around the temple causing ground level to become approximately twenty feet higher than it is now. So in the twentieth century when archaeologists set about excavating Luxor Temple, they cleared away the debris down to the present day ground level, while leaving the Mosque of Abu el Haggag standing in its original position—twenty feet up in the air. It still stands today within the walls of the ancient Luxor Temple and that's why it's necessary to climb all those stairs to get inside it.

The mosque, with the holy man's tomb inside, is visited by thousands of pilgrims each year. Now, tourists are welcome and encouraged to visit. Sixteen years ago when I was enjoying the big parade and festivities that accompany the annual *mulid* of this Saint, outsiders were not encouraged. At that time I wanted to visit the mosque to see the tomb, but I wasn't sure it would be appropriate for me to go there alone. To my amazement, when a group of women from inside the mosque saw me approaching, they ran outside and greeted and welcomed me with open arms. We went inside and I explained that this was my first visit. I received a lovely personal tour and invitations to return. And I have returned often but the warm welcome I receive each time has never equaled the one I received from the women many years ago.

Omran and I journeyed to my favorite Nile-side restaurant and shared a lunch before continuing on to his brother's real estate company, where Omran worked. As we were crossing the street, in gentlemanly fashion, he held out his hand to assist me down from the curb, adding in his improving English, "Give me your leg." How can I walk if he is holding my leg, I wondered. It took me a few seconds to understand what he really meant as I offered him my hand. From there we sailed back across the Nile River, to his home in the village and to my hotel in the village of Birayt. Omran had already invited me to a large wedding in a further village that evening and I was looking forward to cleaning up and wearing the fancy new Egyptian *abaya* (black outer garment) I'd purchased a few days earlier in the local *suq* (market place).

We went on to visit his family home, and had dinner with his mother and three sisters and young nephew. After a village tour and more family introductions, we ended up again in his village coffee house for tea and *shisha* before flagging down a local pick-up truck and climbing into the back end for our taxi to the wedding.

During our time in Omran's home with his mother and sisters and four year-old nephew, I overheard him tell them that he intends to marry me. I just met this guy a few hours ago and hearing that news for the first time put me in a state of shock and caused me to question his sanity and sincerity. When they looked at me, obviously waiting for my response, I simply said, "*InshAllah*" (if God wills it). I love those words in the Arabic language. It is possibly the most used phrase in the language and it has saved me many times. I can never be wrong if I let God do all of the decision making.

We had been together constantly that day for 15 hours, never with a lull in our conversation or laughter. He had a very keen sense of humor and we laughed at the same things. We were totally at ease with each other and I actually wanted to be with him. He kept emphasizing that he felt we had known each other in another life. At that time I couldn't confirm that feeling for myself, although it was obvious that we had an instant and strong connection.

I was out of my hotel an extraordinarily long time that day, and the Amon Hotel staff called me on my mobile phone around midnight to see if I was all right and to make sure I didn't need any help. Nice guys! I really appreciated their attention and caring.

Omran also made it very clear to me that "I am a simple man. I like a simple life." I made a note in my journal that evening that he is "handsome, nice, fun, and smart." I had a strong feeling this would not be the last time I saw Omran, even though I was already ticketed to leave Egypt and return to the United States in two days and those days were already fully scheduled.

One Special Wedding

Our courtship was quite unique, speaking for hours at a time, twice daily, via Skype—I was in America and Omran was in Egypt. Having a long distance romance via the internet was a new experience for both of us. Never had I dreamed I'd have daily communication with one of the oldest areas of the world, using the most advanced equipment available, even though he used the local internet café. I label our courtship as *intense*. We each sat about eighteen inches from the computer screen, looking directly at the other and giving our undivided attention for a solid hour or more each day—or twice daily—with no interruptions. In my opinion, that *is* intense. I had no idea that two people could actually fall in love via the internet, but it happened!

Often times, Omran called via Skype to invite me to have tea with him. We each left the computer and made ourselves tea then sat down and drank it together. Having the camera as a tool also gave us the opportunity to meet and visit with each other's family and friends. I gave him a tour of my home in America and even showed him the view outside my windows. He saw falling snow for the first time and the green grass and tall trees of a golf course. Occasionally he and I met for lunch together, in the same way we met for tea. Yes, we had fallen in love.

While I enjoy all village weddings, there is one that especially stands out as lovely and beautiful and great fun: my own! As soon as I chose a date to leave America and return to Luxor, Omran began planning our wedding.

It took place two days after my arrival back in Luxor, on the West Bank, in his village, in the courtyard and garden of his family home. He engaged the musicians, and hired men to clean and groom the garden, purchased the soft drinks, secured the food for the women of the family to prepare, ordered a new galabaya of very good quality fabric for himself, and told everyone he knew that his wedding would be Saturday night. He also rented a lovely big house with a beautiful garden for our residence, in a near-by village. All this while going twice to the airport, as I missed my connections to Luxor and had to overnight in Cairo.

I kept emphasizing that I wanted a small wedding and he kept assuring me that it would be small. I requested that he wear a *galabaya*—the traditional long flowing every day garment worn by the men and women of Egypt—and I would wear a fancy *galabaya* myself. A *galabaya* for the bride and groom is most unorthodox. All brides want the white traditional western style wedding dress but I wanted to dress Egyptian style. I had spent the day helping the women prepare the wedding feast and the July heat didn't permit make-up to stay in place, so I attended my own wedding with my hair in a ponytail and absolutely no make-up and wearing a borrowed dress—an elegant pink galabaya that caught the lights just right to make it sparkle.

As for wanting a "small" wedding, I learned that in the mind of Omran, "small" meant a one-day wedding celebration rather than a four-day traditional event. At least two hundred of his family and close friends came to help us celebrate well into the morning hours. The women all sat on one side of the court yard and all the men sat on the opposite side, with the band and singer in the center.

As with any social activity, the longer the party, the more lively and loose it becomes and that's when the best dancing takes place. According to the Holy Quran, the use of alcohol is forbidden for Muslims, but I always suspect that as the evening goes on, some of the Cokes and Fantas might be tampered with and enhanced a bit with the forbidden *juice.*

Village weddings are well attended by the children, with a special area designated for their seating. I've never seen a child misbehaving at one of these weddings but I've seen plenty of children lying on the ground, sleeping through the activities.

Lover's Quarrel

We had little in common. We shared different languages, different cultures, different religions, different education, and different tastes in food. I really couldn't find anything that we did have in common—except for the love and passion that we shared and our sense of humor. As newlyweds, Omran and I had some very serious and heated disagreements. We never argued or disagreed about the major things or important things in our lives. We were in perfect harmony about the big things. Our first conflict was about how long to boil the eggs for eating. He said thirty minutes at a rolling boil and I wanted a three minute egg. He said I would die if I ate a three minute egg. I said in thirty minutes his egg would turn to powder. We each ate our egg *our way* to prove our point. This argument was so serious it almost caused us to split.

The second disagreement came about because I wanted to put a sweet potato in the soup pot. *Everyone* knows you can't cook something sweet with something salted, he told me. Would this old wives tale ruin an otherwise beautiful relationship? It almost did!

In the midst of another very big disagreement, I said, "I'm not talking to you anymore," and turned to walk away. At that time my cell phone rang so I answered. Yes, it was Omran, standing about eight feet from me and we continued our argument standing in the same room, back to back, talking to each other on our cell phones. We both ended up in giggles, as usually happens when we argue. It's very difficult to express anger through laughter. Someday, I keep telling myself, we will have a disagreement about something that really matters, but so far it hasn't happened. We will keep trying, I'm sure!

Om Gozi

I am the only person who can call her "Om Gozi." No one else can
address her by that title. "Om" is the Arabic word for "mother." In
the old days, and still in many areas of Egypt, a woman did not want her
given name known, and after she married she should never be addressed
by her given name. Married women are known by and addressed by the
given name of their first born son. Thus, Omran's mother is known as
"Om Omran" (Mother of Omran). However, Omran and his sisters call
her "Omi" or "my mother."

But I find Om Omran difficult to say, so I address her as "Om Gozi"
or "Mother of my husband." I don't even know her name. I like this
woman. In fact, I adore this woman! This is a relationship I can't begin
to describe, though I have no problem understanding it. It's the love
between two women whose hearts and spirits walk on the same path.
The heart can and does speak. I can rarely understand her speech as she
talks in a very old dialect. She doesn't understand a word of English.
So how do we communicate? I think there are just some things that all
women understand and share.

She has a wonderful sense of humor. I can tell by the way her eyes
dance and her lips curl upward with a smile as she approaches me with a
story to tell. In the same manner, I can tell when things are not going her
way. I love it when she tells me the family news and gossip. Sometimes I
feel free to pass this information to Omran and together we can usually

determine where to go for a complete story, if need be. But when she whispers to me a family secret, I can tell by the change in her tone that this should not go any further and I honor that! She is proud of me and likes for me at accompany her to village social events. Once after Omran and I had a small disagreement, she took him aside and gave him a royal scolding! She had no idea what our disagreement involved or if anyone should be considered at fault. No one, not even Om Gozi, knows her age.

There are no official papers or government registrations to verify her birth. She was born in a time and place that didn't consider the birth of a girl to have much importance. She never had an opportunity for education so she cannot read or write. She lives today in the same village where she was born. If she could count, she could probably count on two hands the number of times in her life she has visited Luxor, a few miles directly across the river—and that is usually to visit a family member in the hospital.

It was a family decision that she should marry her first cousin at a very early age, probably around fourteen years. The entire family was devastated when about five years later she was left a widow with three young children. At that time there were no provisions for support for a widow—except from the family. In time, she married a very good man; a widower with three young children. Together they added four more, bringing the total living off-spring in the home to ten.

Just in the past few months she made her first trip to Cairo to visit her newly married daughter, the first of her children to leave the village. Her second trip into the Cairo world was with Omran and me. For Om Gozi, it was her first time to ride in a first class rail car—with padded seats, adjustable backs and a foot rest! And hot tea available for purchase. I had packed a healthy supply of snacks and sandwich preparations for the twelve hour journey. Omran is Om Gozi's youngest child and the only male in this part of the family. Sadly, his father died when he was just sixteen years of age so this made Omran the man of the family. The responsibility of caring for his elderly mother and his mature unmarried sisters often weighs heavily on Omran.

My mother-in-law took me aside and whispered her request: would I color her hair before the big feast day? Black, of course. Now, this is a woman who for more than sixty years has been covered in layer upon layer of black fabric from head to toe. No one outside her immediate family has seen her hair during this time—and very few inside the family. She even wears her hijab while sleeping. My first thought: maybe I misunderstood her Arabic. Surely she did not say that she wanted her hair colored. But my sisters-in-law confirmed that I had understood correctly. So, the day before the great feast, I arrived at her home with a box of hair color which I had made a special trip to Luxor to seek out and buy. She was thrilled with her switch from all white hair to black and after her daughters and I heaped compliments on her, and even before it was dry, she put her black head coverings back on and, with a sly little smile; she went about her daily routine, fully confident of her beauty—which no one could see but she knew to be true.

Now, I don't want to make this operation sound too simple. My mother-in-law's home is one of those mud-brick houses with no plumbing, so in order to rinse the coloring agent from her hair we had to first build a fire in the courtyard, and then heat a large pan of water which was carried from the outdoor hydrant. She then knelt on the ground on all fours, with her head over an empty basin and I mixed the warm and cold water until it was a comfortable temperature and poured it over her hair again and again until the water ran clear of color.

It's Madame Omran

When ferry passengers alight on the west bank from Luxor, there is a mad rush toward the public transportation vehicles. The pick-up trucks with the wooden benches in the back and the vans with the doors permanently fixed open fill up very fast and take off immediately. The river crossing on the ferry provides only the first half of the journey home.

As the last vehicle going in my direction was pulling away from the terminal, I noted that it was completely full. I was not looking forward to the wait for another one, so my spirits lifted when I heard someone from inside the back end of the pick-up truck yell, "Stop, stop! It's Madame Omran (wife of Omran)." The truck braked and all twelve men inside instantly rearranged themselves to make ample room for me. It would not have been appropriate for me to sit so that any part of my body touched one of the men. I knew none of the men in that truck, but apparently someone knew Omran. Each man greeted me politely with downcast eyes but there was no conversation coming my way. When I relayed this story to Omran, his comment was, "You see, it pays to always be nice to everyone, because you never know when or how it will come back to you." This is one of his philosophies for living his life. On another occasion, in an offhand manner I said to Omran, "Why are you always so nice to that man? He's a terrible person."

Omran's comment put me in my place; "Yes, I know he's a terrible person, but I am not." There surely are people in the world who could match Omran for his honesty and integrity and his wholesome clean approach to life, but I doubt that one could be found who could surpass him.

Eid El Adha

Everyone shared in the excitement of the approaching religious feast days. Eid el Adha occurs seventy days after Ramadan, and like all religious feasts it's a time for visiting family and friends and for getting new clothes. Although the name really means The Feast of the Sacrifice, it seems that no one sacrifices when it comes to new clothing and good food for the event. Eid el Adha celebrates an event that is important in the three major religions—it recalls and celebrates Abraham's willingness to sacrifice his son Isaac when God requested it. Instead, God saved Isaac, and father Abraham sacrificed a ram instead. This story is recorded in the Torah, Old Testament and the Quran, however the son being offered up is referenced as Ismail in the Quran.

It is common for those who can afford to do so to sacrifice an animal in thanksgiving for their own blessings—or maybe to make a request. It is a long standing tradition in the Muslim world that one third of the slaughtered animal be given to loved ones of choice, one third must be given to the poor and the last third is kept and enjoyed by those making the sacrifice. Omran and I had decided to become business partners and we opened a very small restaurant on a Luxor side street. Things were going well and we were enjoying an average degree of success. We served strictly home-style Egyptian food and most of our business came from our local friends and neighbors.

When a person has a special reason for thanksgiving to Allah (God), or if there is a special favor to be asked, and providing one can afford it, the sacrifice of a healthy, non-pregnant animal during Eid el Adha is in keeping with the teachings of Islam. Omran and I were very thankful for our restaurant and its success. For a couple weeks, he discussed with me his desire to thank Allah with a sacrificial offering. The cost of buying a healthy, adult sheep was about three and a half months wages for the average Egyptian! For Omran, that cost made the purchase impossible. In order to make this sacrifice, one must be a very successful man. After a considerable amount of time in my own prayer and meditation, I felt that I wanted to share the cost of purchasing the sheep and, Omran said I also would be a participant in this sacrificial offering. I wasn't sure that would be acceptable for a non-Muslim. But if my heart were in a good place, how could it possibly be anything but right! My husband and I were thanking God together.

The sacrifice of an animal is not an act done in private or behind closed doors. The sacrifice of animals is an important occurrence and it usually takes place in a conspicuous public place and all the men are welcome to be present and participate. It is not considered an unclean act, nor is any part of the animal considered unclean. Therefore, no one is squeamish about blood and guts and long after the sacrifice, there's still no hurry to clean the area. There is typically a large gathering of male family, friends and passersby to assist in the preparation, or simply to enjoy the company of one another. It's a social event and a religious event. Women don't participate—that's not a religious rule but rather it is custom. I was made to feel very welcome. As always, in Egypt, male children are a big part of such events. This is how the father teaches his sons about such things and there's much for the sons to learn.

There is a specific manner in which the killing of the animal must be done. One cannot speak about killing the animal in the presence of that animal, or any live animal. The animal must be killed with one clean cut to the throat with a very sharp knife. But, the animal—or any live animal—must not see the knife. An animal must be treated with kindness. Always, the animal must face toward Makka, the holy city in

Saudi Arabia and, as he makes the fatal cut, the butcher must call out, *"Allahu Akhbar"* (God is great). Even a housewife killing a chicken for dinner must follow these rules.

On the chosen day, Omran was up early, bathed, shaved, dressed in his new western style feast-day clothes, and out the door, on his way to our restaurant. I was much less enthusiastic, taking a long bath, shampooing and drying my hair, staring blankly into my closet, not knowing just what would be proper to wear to this event. When in doubt I always chose something conservative. I wore a plain skirt, a loose plain color blouse with long sleeves and of course, my hair was covered in the traditional style. I was very properly dressed. As I neared completion of my morning ritual, Omran rushed back into the apartment and commanded that I must hurry. "All the people are ready and waiting, but I told them they cannot begin until you arrive. *Yalla! Yalla*! (Hurry! Hurry!) I had to run to keep up with him as we made our way to the restaurant.

The crowd of about thirty men, waiting in the street in front of our restaurant was quite relieved to see me arrive. Imagine, a woman—a foreign woman—holding up an important religious ritual, a special thanksgiving to Allah! The prayers and activities were about to begin and all the people were ready. With great ceremony, our chef was sharpening his knife behind the tethered sheep and the men had decided who would do each task. The extra pots were in place to hold all the parts of the animal. The water was already boiling. Everything was set to go! The anticipation ran very high. The sacrifice was going to take place in the street and the crowd had already swelled to such numbers that it formed a barrier wall.

The group parted when I arrived to make room for me to enter. I walked toward the sheep, tethered there in the street in front of the restaurant and patted him between his magnificent horns, caressed his wooly back, and affectionately put my arms around his neck and hugged him. In a weakening, but still clear voice, through my breaking tears, I said "No, Omran, you can't do this! You cannot kill this beautiful animal." Gasps of horrified disbelief came from the crowd. I had just told my husband he could not make this offering of thanks to Allah. Did I not acknowledge God? Did I have no fear of God? Calling on the same patient reserve he had been forced to use on previous occasions, Omran had to once again calm the crowd and explain the actions of his American wife—the wife who spoke to her husband as an equal—the wife who dared to disagree and say so—the wife who was not Muslim—the wife who honored and respected the Egyptian ways—and the only wife present. As heads began slowly nodding up and down, and furrowed brows began to smooth, the men in turbans and galabayas were acknowledging that they understood his words but they could not readily accept them.

I could not leave this situation in limbo and I, too, had to understand and accept. I had to understand that this sacrifice was a blessing and an honor they and their father's fathers had shared for generations. They were acting out a ritual of supreme love and obedience for *Allah* (God), just as Abraham had when he was ready to answer God's call to slay his own son. Humbly, I turned to my husband and said, "It's okay. Go ahead." But I also had to honor my own feelings of sadness for the loss of God's creature standing before me. I silently said my goodbyes to the sacrificial sheep and bade him to go to the wonderful green pastures with abundant running water on the other side. Then I breathed a prayer of thanksgiving that many people would enjoy the feast provided by this beautiful animal. I lowered my head and walked alone to an area where I couldn't see the action, and as the religious fervor reached a higher pitch, so did the tears spilling profusely down my cheeks.

After the sacrificial animal is properly bled, it is customary for the person making the sacrifice to dip the right hand in the fresh warm blood and make an imprint on the outer wall of the building or dwelling. Omran and I did this together. Our prints were visible for many months and served as a reminder to all who saw them that these persons had much to be thankful for. I see a little prestige attached to this action also. As for me, now everyone in the neighborhood learned that I had a soft spot in my heart for animals. From that day, whenever my name is mentioned, the people say, "Ah, Madame Omran. She has the heart of a child." I think that is a good thing.

The Traffic Light

Walking home one evening I noticed that a traffic light was being installed at a little used intersection. Bicycles and donkey carts use this intersection more than automobiles. Government waste often causes me to stress, and this traffic light was completely uncalled for. By the time I reached our restaurant I was pretty worked up and I ranted to Omran. He listened politely and when I finished, he simply looked at me and with a shrug of the shoulders, in typical Egyptian fashion, unsmiling he said, "Don't worry. It's just for decoration."

He was absolutely right! Six years later the light was still hanging there, never having been in operation. It *was* just for decoration.

Ramadan and Eid El Fitur

*R*amadan is a word that most non-Muslims have heard. In the Islamic religion there is a lunar calendar that has 12 months, but it is ten to twelve days shorter than the solar calendar and is followed by all Muslims for religious purposes. For most other purposes they follow the Gregorian calendar, which seems a bit confusing to a non-Muslim. Ramadan is the name of one of the months in the Islamic calendar—the ninth month. Because the calendar is lunar, the months change as the moon dictates the time of the year for the ninth month. The ninth month was chosen as the holy month because this is the time that God revealed the scriptures of the Holy Quran to the Prophet Mohamed (PBUH). When writing the name of the prophet, it is customary for Muslims to always add the letters PBUH behind the name, which stand for Peace Be Upon Him.

Ramadan might come during the summer or the winter because it follows the lunar calendar. There is great excitement and anticipation in the air the day before Ramadan begins. It seems like everyone is watching the sky, looking for the *hilal* (crescent) moon to appear, thus indicating the beginning of the holy month. One can't know exactly when the month begins until the moon tells them.

The month of Ramadan is the most sacred time in the Islamic calendar. During this month, all Muslims are bound to follow certain fasting rules and certain rules of other abstinence. It is intended to be a time of prayer and extra devotion, of sacrifice, of generosity to the poor or those in need. Between the hours of sunrise and sunset, there should be no food or liquid consumed no use of tobacco, no sexual activity. Ramadan is observed with different additional traditions in each country or region.

Just as we in the west wish others a Merry Christmas, here in Upper Egypt the typical Ramadan greeting is *"Ramadan Karim"* meaning Ramadan is generous. People of other countries may give a different Ramadan greeting.

Sunset, the time for breaking the fast, occurs at a slightly different time each day. A family might sit gathered around the food for several minutes, waiting for the signal that the sun has officially set and it is time to begin eating. In Egypt, that message is announced on the television, from the minaret of most mosques and by the booming sound of a cannon being fired. At that moment, all eighty-six million of Egypt's residents have begun to eat *iftar,* the break-the-fast meal, often simply called break-fast. This is possibly where our word *breakfast* comes from. We are breaking our over-night fast.

I always think it is amusing when I'm in a restaurant during this time and every hungry restaurant patron is sitting with a plate full of food in from of him. Then everyone in the room, after a full day of fasting, begins eating at the exact same time.

Egyptians look forward to this time of fasting with great enthusiasm. It is not to be dreaded. All year long there are remembrances to Ramadan, much like Christmas is remembered in the west. Amongst the official exceptions to the fasting rule is a dispensation for pregnant woman or ill persons or those traveling. Children decide for themselves when they are ready to fast, but with loving encouragement from parents and other family members. Some children begin by partially fasting.

As a non-Muslim, I am often asked if I intend to fast during Ramadan. I love being in Egypt during this time, and yes, I do observe the fast. Because of the generous and social nature of the Egyptian people, I cannot recall an evening when I was not invited to join another family for this special meal. For this, I am very grateful. But for me, it is more than a time for holding back on the food. It is a very spiritual time for me and I love the energy that fills the air and fills me. It would not be possible to ignore this. Everyone is loving and caring and this type of energy causes the hearts and spirits of many to overflow. I'm actually grateful to make extra time for prayer and meditation.

When I was spending a week in Cairo during Ramadan, the management of the hotel where I was staying invited me to join all the staff for their special daily *iftar*. The elaborate meal was prepared each Ramadan day by the hotel management, especially for the staff. These folks had been working very hard all day with no food or drink. I felt quite honored to have been invited to join them—and the only hotel guest or non-Muslim to be in attendance.

Outside of certain business establishments, or indeed, outside of some homes, a special table is set up in the street and laden with food. Those who have no family or no opportunity to join a family are welcome to come to this table any day or every day. No one should go without these special Ramadan meals.

Another Ramadan tradition that is similar to one of ours in the West is decorating with colored electric lights. Lights are strung from the minarets of mosques, and from other buildings and private balconies. One year during my time in Egypt, Christmas fell during the time of Ramadan and I decided to honor my own tradition by decorating my balcony with colored lights. All my friends and neighbors congratulated me profusely because they thought I had really gotten into the spirit of Ramadan. Actually, I was in the spirit of Ramadan even though I was decorating for myself and my own holiday.

Ramadan days are slow and lazy. Most people stay close to home, sleeping as much as possible and when awake, they are as inactive as possible. All eating establishments are closed, coffee houses and food shops are closed except those that sell necessary items for the iftar (break-fast meal). Egypt is reasonably quiet during these daylight hours.

Because Ramadan is so special, the very word has taken on expanded meaning. In addition to being the name of the ninth month, Ramadan is also a favorite given name for Egyptian males, for commercial enterprises, for street names, and even for a new city.

After sundown the fully nourished and fully rested Egyptians are ready to play again. And do they play! Most families dress up and go visiting other families. Many go to a government sponsored club for socializing, soft drinks, and to let the children enjoy the playground equipment or the rides. Others involve themselves in soccer games. For many it is now time for shopping. Teenagers simply walk the streets, wanting to see and be seen.

The government sponsored a series of live entertainments in the new plaza beside Luxor Temple and Abu el Haggag Mosque. Every night thousands of people came to be professionally entertained at one of the five temporary stages. Many people picnicked in the grassy areas and simply enjoyed people watching or drinking tea or Coca Cola. It was a wonderful social atmosphere as one was bound to see old friends or make new ones. Every night the music and dancing continued until around one-thirty or two o'clock in the morning. I think we attended every evening, often taking one of Omran's sisters or his nephew with us.

The mosque of Abu el Hagagg, built inside Luxor Temple, remained open until late into the night with a constant parade of people going inside to honor the twelfth century holy man. On my own numerous visits, a high priority for me was to also view and study the recent restoration of the building. Since few people are interested in this phase of the mosque, the guards and attendants were more than happy to unlock doors and turn on lights for me—and to offer explanations.

It isn't that all people look forward to the end of Ramadan, but rather that all people look forward to the three day feast that immediately follows Ramadan, Eid el Fitur. If anyone didn't get enough socializing during Ramadan, he can certainly catch up during the feast. During this time many families travel to other parts of Egypt to visit loved ones. Some choose this time for holiday activities such as visiting the many resort regions of Egypt. One very important traditional aspect of this feast is that everyone MUST have some new article of clothing to wear and show off. As the fast nears its conclusion, the shops and stores become somewhat of a madhouse with everyone trying to purchase the finest and most beautiful garment for the lowest price they can negotiate.

If visiting family and friends was important during Ramadan, it becomes a thousand times more important during the feast. I am still baffled that everyone is out visiting, but every time we call on someone, they are at home accepting visitors. Somehow it works. No matter where in the world one happens to be, parading about adorned in new clothing makes one feel attractive and special. On the first day of the feast every Egyptian is dressed in his or her new clothing. Little girls are the cutest to watch as they strut. They *know* they are pretty and they want to be sure that everyone else knows it too.

Merry Donkey Ride

One of the activities that gave me much pleasure was riding a donkey into the hills and mountains. A mountain in Egypt's *sahara* (desert) is nothing like the Alps, but it is a high pile of sand and rocks, eroded from years of flash floods and wind. It looks a little like a miniature Grand Canyon. This mountain stands high above the Valley of the Kings, burial site of many of Egypt's ancient royal families. You will never see a blade of grass—or anything green—on this mountain. Small animals scamper about, hiding under and behind rocks, looking for something to eat. I have often seen friendly apparitions moving about in this area. I welcome this. I feel they are there for my protection. I have never seen a snake or scorpion in these rocks.

I put great trust in the surefootedness of my little donkey when I'm riding there. Sometimes the trail is so steep and narrow it is necessary to get off the donkey and walk alone. I rarely used a saddle when my donkey and I got together. A blanket across his back and a simple bridle were easiest but definitely not the safest way to travel. Stirrups weren't used and my dangling legs often rubbed or banged against the stone walls, throwing me completely off balance. I've taken my share of tumbles. My donkey actually belonged to friends in the village, who made it clear that I could use this animal at anytime without even asking them.

In the quiet of one beautiful late afternoon, I was riding in this area, very much at peace with myself and the entire world. As I looked about at the exquisite beauty of Mother Nature's creations and my surroundings, I said to myself, "I bet no one knows of this place—just God and me." I had barely completed the thought when I noticed a man walking on the narrow trail, coming toward me.

As he got closer I could see that he was an Asian man; a tourist same as me. (In Egypt, any person who is not Egyptian, no matter how long they have lived here or where they are from is considered a tourist.) When he got close enough for eye contact, he gave me a happy smile and very graciously said, "Merry Christmas" in perfect English. I was almost too stunned to reply. I did not know this date was December 25, Christmas Day in the west and Christmas Day for me.

This simple and pleasant memory is engrained forever. I wondered how he knew to wish me a Merry Christmas. Chances are good that he was not even of the Christian religion. How did he know that I would be one to acknowledge Christmas on this day? Just because I'm white does not mean that I honor Christmas on this day. Many Europeans, South Americans, and Egypt's Coptic Christians celebrate Christmas in January. I could have been one of them. How did he know I would understand English? I could have been from Europe and not understood any language except my own.

I am very grateful that he did let me know it was December 25 and that he shared the season's greeting with me. After I left the mountain and fed and watered my donkey, and settled him into his resting place, I hurried to my flat across the river and phoned all my family in America to wish them a very merry Christmas. I would have been quite upset with myself if I had failed to wish Christmas greetings to my loved ones.

De Nile or Denial

My son Jeffrey came from America to visit me and I very much looked forward to spending time with him and showing him *my* Egypt. He is the only family member who shares my interest in travel and in ancient history. We spent two weeks getting to know the Upper Egyptian people and exploring ruins, often hiring a private guide if I didn't feel I had adequate knowledge about the antiquity we were planning to visit that day.

Jeffrey and I are both nature enthusiasts and enjoy being out-of-doors and active, so the River Nile captured our attention. The world's longest river enters Egypt from the south after passing through eight other African countries. The Blue Nile and the White Nile converge at Khartoum in the Sudan, creating one magnificent body of water over four thousand miles in length. Without this river cutting through the center of the land, the desert that is Egypt might never have developed into the extraordinary civilization that it became.

As our minds focused on the illustrations painted in tombs and cut into the stone temple walls, we became more and more aware that the Nile no longer had the same characteristics as those shown us from ancient times. Gone today are the swamps where tomb paintings reveal that Pharaoh and his hunting parties searched for birds. Gone are the papyrus fields that stretched as far as the eye could see and provided the ancients with a most valuable material. Without this abundant plant it's possible that we would have no written records of life in this area three thousand five hundred years ago. The fauna also had changed dramatically. Wall carvings show us that a huge population of crocodiles and hippopotami claimed large areas of the Nile for themselves. Lions and ostriches lived in the wild in Pharaonic times but all are now extinct in Egypt. We wanted to see the Nile as the ancients knew it. Was this possible?

Over the years I read numerous times that there were places in east Africa where the Nile does, indeed, resemble the river as it was many years earlier, so Jeffrey and I decided to travel to Kenya, Tanzania, and Uganda to have a look for ourselves. We connected with a travel company that provided a good-sounding trip and at a very reasonable price—probably because we were transported in the back end of an open truck sitting on wood benches and pitched our own one-person tents nightly in the African bush. We enjoyed the luxury of our own native driver, cook, guide, and armed guard. Jeffrey and I were in seventh heaven!

When our small group transferred to a little, rather rickety, ten-passenger motorized ferry boat for the trip upriver to Uganda's spectacular Murchison Falls, I was overflowing with excitement. Some call this the headwaters of the Nile. Finding a passage through the infestation of Nile Crocodiles and families of hippos, lounging both in the water beside us and on the sunny river banks, was very frightening. It would have been easy for a croc to jump onboard or for a hippo to upset us from below. Here on the Victorian branch of the Nile, my fears quickly turned to unbelievable amazement when I got my first glimpse of the spectacular fall, shooting through the twenty foot wide crevice and dropping frothing white water four hundred feet in three cascades. Except for the waterfall, all around me looked like the pictures I'd seen on the ancient walls of Egypt, including those green papyrus fields as far as I could see. Now this was the Nile and this was what I traveled to Uganda to see. What a thrill.

We disembarked and began climbing the steep rocky path to the top of the falls, where our bus would meet us. It didn't appear particularly challenging so I charged ahead, though feeling a great lack of energy and overwhelmed with exhaustion. I was the first to hit the trail but the last to reach the top. I had to sit down to rest six times on the way up. This wasn't like me at all. I was in excellent physical condition—or was I? At dinner that evening I did not join in the conversation, but I had a new experience: I fell asleep sitting in my chair at the table, my face almost going directly into my soup bowl as my head dropped. Oh, I was tired and feeling feverish, but I was also looking forward to our upcoming night crossing of Lake Victoria.

The group adventure ended and Jeff and I were on our way to an ocean-side resort in Mombasa to rest a bit after our month-long camp-out. Despite having nausea and throwing up now, I still was looking forward to the resort and then returning to my apartment in Luxor. I sat in the background, unable to be of any help, as Jeffrey checked us into the resort. Our room for the next week would be a luxurious round, thatched, African style hut that had a tub and shower, television, and beds with mattresses.

When I tried to speak, the words came out in an incoherent jumble. The desk clerk noticed me and firmly spoke to Jeffrey. "Your mother is a very sick woman. You need to get her to a doctor as quickly as possible. I will call a taxi now." Like the desk clerk, the physician took one look at me and made his diagnosis: malaria. Malaria claims the life of 2.1 million persons annually, but none of us on the tour had recognized the signs, as we all came from countries where this illness has been eradicated. My temperature had reached 107 degrees and the doctor said that if I had come to him two days later, he could not have done anything for me. I would have died in Kenya. Even though I was fulfilling my dream of exploring the ancient Nile, I truly was in denial about being so ill. After a week of daily injections I was strong enough to board the airplane and return home to Luxor, though quite unsteady and still confused. It took a year to completely recover. I am thankful to be alive.

East Side, West Side: New Flat in the City

Living in a remote small desert village on the west side of the Nile was a new experience for me, as my previous years of living in Egypt had involved city life. I loved having a large house with a beautiful garden full of flowering shrubs and tall trees, most of which gave forth delicious fruits—and a gardener to care for it all. It was invigorating to have a house sitting on the edge of the great Sahara and to enjoy life somewhat as it was lived a hundred or two hundred years ago. But when I wanted to sit down and be served a cup of tea, or make a quick trip to the pharmacy, or have a restaurant meal, or simply go window shopping, it could not be done in my remote area.

So I decided I wanted to enjoy the conveniences of life in town for a while. Omran had never lived anyplace outside his small village and it took a bit of convincing to sell him on the idea of city life. But he was a good sport and did a good job of choosing a Luxor city flat for us. It was satisfactory but needed a good cleaning. All my women friends and family offered to come and help. Our flat was in the neighborhood where I lived sixteen years ago so I felt quite comfortable, even with all the changes that had taken place. I had girlfriends in that area and the best shopping was there.

In ancient times when Luxor was Egypt's capital, it was a beautiful city but today I could not find one residential street in the town of Luxor that I considered attractive, nor could I find one dwelling that I thought was architecturally appealing. Buildings look like ugly boxes with walls made of a single stack of bricks. The outside walls were never finished and rarely painted. Because the government does not collect taxes on unfinished buildings, there is little incentive to complete construction. Staircases are solid cement and most buildings are four to five stories tall. There are no single-family dwellings in the towns or cities of Egypt and all buildings are attached to the next one in line, with no spaces between them. In the west we call these row houses. So each street looks just the same as the street before it and after it. Every apartment in the building has windows in the front, or street side, and any windows on the interior open to an air shaft; therefore I could smell what my neighbors upstairs and downstairs were cooking for dinner. Sometimes the smell of two separate dinners cooking was compatible and made me hungry, but more often it was unpleasantly overwhelming.

Each flat, had a miniature brick balcony at the front, allowing the occupants to observe the neighbors and the street action below. The balcony was rarely wide enough to place a chair there. Attached to every balcony, as if required, were the clothes lines. One stood on the balcony and leaned out over the street below to hang the laundry on the clothes lines.

A woman cannot hang her underwear where it can be seen and it is often dried in a private place inside the house, if indeed there is such a space. But this custom simply presented a fun challenge for me and I tried to determine how many different ways I could hide or disguise my undies while they hung on the clothesline outside, over the street. Not only could someone look up from the street and see them, but someone from a higher balcony could look down and see them, I was told by the neighbor women. So this was one of the ways I entertained myself on laundry day. Sometimes I literally laughed out loud at my creativity and silliness. My favorite was to make a tunnel using the freshly laundered sheets, and then put the clean underwear inside the tunnel to dry. I learned to fold a pair of panties in six different shapes so that a viewer could not identify them.

If there was a sidewalk between the building and the street it was no wider than two and a half feet and was usually broken and crumbling and unusable, the result of using poor quality building materials. There was never a lawn, or even a patch of dirt, between the building and the sidewalk. Streets were very narrow, just wide enough for two automobiles to pass if done very carefully and if the rear-view mirrors were folded against the automobiles rather than protruding. On very rare occasion an owner may have planted a tree in the middle of the sidewalk, but I never saw grass or flowers. This is the *sahara*.

There were no supermarkets at the time, so having a chicken for dinner meant that I first had to find the lady standing in a shady spot (if there was one) with her stack of caged live birds. If I asked her kindly and tipped her well, she would graciously sever the chick's head, thus I could take home a dead chicken. Then I had to pluck it, singe the tiny feathers off, gut it, and then cut it into serving pieces. When I finished this little chore the first time, I asked my neighbor how I should dispose of the left-over mess. "Oh, just throw it over your balcony into the street and the stray cats will eat it." There's no way I could throw a bag of chicken feathers, guts, severed feet and head, etc. over the balcony, but I carefully wrapped this package and carried it downstairs. Then I walked down the street to the last building in our row, tip-toed to the back of the building and very gently laid my package on the ground, thinking that sooner or later a cat might find it. Before I could even raise my head and straighten my body, I heard a loud "Whoosh!" and the package was gone. It happened so fast, I merely saw a blur of action in front of me. I don't even know how many cats there were. They must have smelled me coming. After that, when I asked my neighbors for advice, I followed their recommendations.

I find it difficult to understand how the Egyptian people can accept or tolerate some of the unpleasant conditions I've mentioned. The interior of an Egyptian home is always very clean, as are their bodies and their clothing.

I've commented previously about the humor I find in the English language signage here. There's a new men's clothing store going in nearby and a great big sign in the window says "New born men's store." I guess that *would* advertise that the store had not been there in the past.

One unusual aspect of this new flat was that it was on the third floor, above a mosque; all the more reason to hide my line-drying underwear. This meant that I heard everything that happened in the mosque and it is a very active place. The call to prayer, the sermons and the men praying inside the mosque kept up a steady rumble throughout the day. On Friday, the holy day, the mosque overflowed with men, so at the appointed time, the younger boys went into the street that ran in front of the mosque and in front of my flat, and they laid large woven mats on the ground. As the crowd from the mosque spilled into the street, the men took their places and spread their own prayer rugs on the mats in the street, and got busy with their prayers. For me, this meant that during the Friday service, I could not come or go from my apartment. I could not get in or out of my building door and even if I could have, I certainly would not have walked among the praying men. This was only a minor inconvenience, given that I liked hearing the sounds of the men praying. Though I could not understand their chanting, the atmosphere overflowed with reverence and I often joined them in my own prayer in the privacy of my flat, just above them.

Our television provided excellent pictures on the two hundred-plus channels we got. One of those was CNN, but it came from the UK, even though there was a fair amount of US news, especially political news. I was fascinated with the television reception and programming, as I think every country in Africa was represented, as well as all the Middle East countries, Asia, India and all those "stan" countries I can't spell. Even the advertising was entertaining.

Saudi Arabia had an excellent documentary type program in good English every day. This was quite an education for me—hearing all these different languages. It also seemed quite unique to see programs from Iraq and Iran television. So far I've never seen a female on Saudi television, unless it's a special program for women, such as a cooking show. Program hosts on Saudi television must be the most handsome men in the country, or maybe they are so enchanting because of the red and white checkered shemagh they wear over their heads while doing their show.

I enjoyed watching the camel races from Dubai, especially since I've followed the trials and tribulations of this sport since Dubai got into trouble with the human rights folks for buying very young boys from poor country families to ride these racing animals. Sometimes the jockey was tied onto the back of the camel. These days, the "jockey" is a specially designed little robotic rider box that is strapped to the camel back and is operated by a person who is in a special area off the race track. It does not give the camel an electric shock but provides the same type of physical stimulation that the rider with his whip would—they say.

I was unable to get the internet at home through the usual way, but Omran worked out a deal with a neighbor and one day I saw a cable inching its way along the side of our building, headed toward the window, traveling from the neighbor's flat into ours. We now have internet. In times like that I don't ask questions.

The Gas Cylinder— Embubba

The *embubba* man on his donkey-pulled cart goes past my home at least three times each day, sitting on top of the stack of large gas filled metal cylinders, smoking his cigarettes, and banging his heavy wrench on one of the cylinders. His objective is to make as much noise as possible in order to let all residents know he is in the neighborhood so they can buy an *embubba*. The gas filled cylinder—called *embubba*, connects to our cook stove—called *butujaz* —butane gas—and this allows the fire for preparing our meals and heating our tea water. So when our *embubba* empties and we can no longer use our *butujaz*, it's very important to know just where the *embubba* man is and we send a neighborhood boy to find him, giving the child an Egyptian pound or two for his efforts.

Often times the *embubba* empties and we have a little extra time before the next meal preparation. When we hear the loud metal wrench banging against the metal container, we go to our balcony and wave to him as he comes down the street. The *embubba* man then brings a full cylinder up to our flat, disconnects the empty *embubba*, connects the new one and carries the empty one away, receives his pay and is on his way. It's all so very simple and easy. Simple, that is, until the government cuts the supply of gas cylinders. For reasons I don't understand, periodically there is no gas in the entire town, or in the entire west bank or in the city. There's no work for the *embubba* man or his donkey. This could continue for a week or a month. Imagine the frustration and hardship of families not being able to even heat water.

As you might expect, there develops an underground or black market supply of *embubbas* at a very expensive rate. One may find it necessary to travel a long distance to buy an *embubba*, adding to the cost. Those who depend on the *embubba* for their livelihood have their own private stash, well hidden away. As the supply lowers, prices rise. So, when our *embubba* finished and we could not conveniently replace it, we decided to "wait it out." Though expensive and inconvenient, every time we wanted a cup of tea, we had to dress and go out to a coffee house or restaurant. Cooking was out of the question, so we ate our meals in restaurants or ate cold sandwiches at home.

One day during this time Omran was discussing the issue with his sister on the phone and suddenly his face lit up. He looked at me and exclaimed, "How could we have been so stupid? For what we have spent on buying tea, we could have bought an electric 'round thing' and heated our water and cooked." Of course, he was absolutely correct and we literally raced to dress and rush out to buy our new electric single burner hot plate! It worked beautifully! Now, why didn't I think of that?

No Privacy

Often I joke about the lack of privacy in Egypt. Within the family there are absolutely no secrets. Within the village there are none. Sometimes I think my neighbors know what time I awaken from sleep in the morning.

Just a few days earlier I had arrived in Luxor from a visit back to America and I was on the ferry, crossing to the west bank to visit old friends. I was greeted by a young man I had known from previous visits and after the lengthy traditional welcome, he inquired, "When did you arrive?" Seeing no need to be specific, I said that I don't really remember, and I thought that would be the end of that conversation.

But another young man, whom I did not know and had never seen before, seated at the end of the ferry's upper deck, cupped his hands around his mouth and called out: "Four days ago. You arrived Monday at six-thirty in the morning." He was right! How did he know? Feeling a complete lack of privacy and a little helpless, all I could say was "Thank you."

Which Way Does the American Lady Go?

I had only been in Luxor a few weeks and hardly knew anyone, so when my doorbell rang at 10:30 one night I was a little startled. Then I saw that the caller was the teller from the bank where I had done business earlier in the evening and I was even more startled. Using both English and Arabic he explained that he gave me too much money when I had exchanged dollars for Egyptian pounds earlier and they could not close the bank until he corrected the situation. For me, that was an easy issue to check out. I had not touched the money so all I had to do was count it. He was right and I was happy to return to the bank what rightfully belonged to the bank.

Before he left I had to ask, "How did you know where I live?"

"It easy," he said in his somewhat basic English. "I just walk outside bank and say to people on street, which way for American lady? They show me (pointing) that way, to juice stand. At juice stand, I say, which way American lady go? All people show me same way—down Medina min el Warra Street. At Medina I say again and people tell me go this street. Then I see children and I say where American lady live and they bring me here. No problem, it easy."

Although I did not know the town's people, they knew me.

Social Life in Luxor

I'm learning a lot of new information about Luxor. It becomes a little more attractive each year as local politicians attempt to leave their mark by completing some beautification project. Also, the Supreme Council of Antiquities wants these projects because it encourages the tourists to spend more time in this city.

Every time we are in Luxor we stroll around and sit in the huge plaza or promenade behind Luxor Temple. Sometimes we go to the local, sort-of-upscale "in" place called Snack Time for *shisha* and tea, where we have a beautiful fifth floor view of Luxor Temple, the River, the west bank, all the way to the King's Valley. I have learned where the underground belly dancing is and where locals can buy and drink beer, and where one can engage a prostitute of any persuasion. But visiting family and friends still tops the list as the number one form of social life. Or perhaps, the number one social event is the wedding. Anyone is welcome and it is a great place to meet new friends and to run into long-time pals. For the men, other than visiting the *ghawah*, that is about the extent of the social life in Luxor. There's not even a cinema.

After While Crocodile

Sometimes during the winter it was cool enough in the mornings that my girlfriend and I could take a little walk for exercise and pleasure. No matter what time of the year, the fields and gardens of Egypt are always bountifully beautiful and green, which seems so incongruous because before the field was growing crops it was just a piece of dry desert. It gave me much pleasure and fulfillment to walk along the high banks of the canal, with lush crops on the upper side and water on the lower side of me. I loved watching the bird life and the small animals that made their home close to the water. One particular morning, as we strolled leisurely along, engaged in serious girl-talk, we heard especially loud grunting noises, with a lot of activity and rustling and thrashing about in the thick growing *barsem* (clover) crop to our right. Curious, we slowed our pace a little so that we could see what it was. We had never heard a sound like this.

Charging at full speed out of the clover and coming directly at me, with mouth wide open, was a five-foot long crocodile. The Nile crocodile has earned a reputation for being the most vicious of all crocs. This couldn't be really happening! I froze in my tracks. No matter how hard I tried, my legs wouldn't move. My feet were cemented to the ground. My friend was several steps ahead of me and I could hear nothing except her panic-filled screams. I knew my life was over and the crocodile would devour me on the spot. I couldn't get my breath! I couldn't call for help—there was no one around. I was acutely aware that I was going to die a horrible and extremely painful death. This would be the end of me. How long would it take for me to die? Would the croc start by ripping my limbs from my body or would it just chew me up, bite by bite? This was going to hurt. Please, dear God, make it quick. The reptile was so close it was possible to count its ugly teeth and see how sharp and dirty they were.

The crocodile was in such a rush coming at me that she ran straight across my feet, causing me to lose my balance and fall to the ground. She kept going at full speed, down the steep bank, to the canal; not even giving me a second look. I had just taken about two seconds and mentally prepared myself for death. What happened, I wondered. This was very confusing. When I realized that I was still alive, I lay on the dusty path and sobbed and sobbed—big crocodile tears you might say—between gasping for my breath and shouting out *"il hamdu lil Allah! il hamdu lil Allah!"*. You see, she was off to protect the babies she had left behind. I had gotten between her and her young ones.

This is not an incident that one forgets or puts aside easily. For weeks and weeks I could not get the images out of my mind and I kept thinking about the facts: I know there are no longer crocodiles north of the Aswan Dam, yet I *did* encounter this one. In Pharaonic times crocodiles were revered as gods and were very plentiful along the River Nile, as were hippopotami. But they have all died out and the upstream dam prevents those in the south from traveling north. I kept thinking that the nose of this crocodile was a little more pointed than most crocs I've been close to. But its mouth *was* wide open and it was trying to scare me. As I gave it more thought, it seemed like its tail was slightly different and maybe its legs were just a little longer than other crocodiles I've seen. But it *was* a big one and it *was* moving very fast!

I asked almost everyone in the town of Luxor about this animal and received no helpful information. People kept telling me that, yes; there are still crocodiles along the Nile and in the canals. Finally, several months later, I came into the possession of a magazine that featured an article on the two types of monitor lizards that live in the *sahara* here in

Upper Egypt. The desert monitor is very rare and the water monitor is even rarer. They do their best to avoid humans. The name is a *warren*. *Il hamdu lil Allah!* I learned that it was the rarest of monitors I had encountered and water monitors feed exclusively on fish and vegetation!

Still, I never walked that pathway again.

My Protest

Animals are not given the same respect and good treatment in Egypt that they often are given in the west. The British have established an animal hospital in Luxor and that has made a big difference in the way many of the carriage drivers take care of their horses.

Walking along one of Luxor's busiest streets, I noted a carriage driver whipping his horse, which was acting in a strange manner. The horse just seemed irritated and out of sorts and didn't want to do what the driver requested. It acted as if it wanted to stop all together. As it hurriedly moved along, under the whip, this horse dropped her foal right there in the middle of the street, still hitched to the carriage. At that point, the driver finally stopped and unhitched her and moved mother horse and baby, along with the carriage, to the side of the street. All this was not a pleasant thing for an animal lover to witness.

I had a personal policy that I would not use a carriage and driver that had a malnourished or unhealthy looking horse pulling it. These horse-drawn carriages are used not just for giving tourists a sightseeing tour of Luxor, but they provide basic transportation for the town's citizens. They provide a taxi service, and like all taxis, they queue up and the one in the front takes the next fare.

On this evening, I decided that I would not go in the first carriage and I chose the second in line. Carriage number one had a tired and unhealthy looking horse and I attempted to explain my position, as briefly and politely as possible. Why did I care about a horse, the driver wanted to know and he angrily told me that the condition of his horse was none of my business and that he would get me to wherever I wanted to go. One angry word led to another and as we verbally sparred back and forth, there in the middle of the busy street, a crowd of men gathered and soon swelled to about fifty. Imagine, an Egyptian carriage driver and a woman—a foreign woman—standing almost toe to toe, and yelling insults and accusations to each other. I was so angry that the words were spilling out of my mouth without me giving any thought to planning what I would say next. I had not realized that I could speak Arabic without giving it any thought. Apparently, I was making myself understood.

I guess the crowning insult came when I yelled, "Look at you. You are fat (he *was* fat) and healthy. Your horse is sick and skinny. You should be down here pulling this carriage and your horse should be sitting up there driving it." The crowd roared and the driver was so enraged and insulted that I honestly feared for my life. I could tell by the expression in his face, had there not been so many people around, he would have killed me on the spot. I could not figure how I would get out of this alive and my trembling body had broken out with huge sweat beads. I was in over-my-head. All this because of a skinny horse?

At that point I could hear fast running footsteps pounding the pavement, coming toward us, and a crazy sounding yelling man bursting through the crowd, making a lot of commotion as he did so. Suddenly all the attention of the crowd was shifted to this crazy yelling man. Someone had seen that I was up-to-my eyeballs in trouble and had gone for Omran. Once he caught his breath, he asked me to tell him exactly what had happened. Successfully holding back my tears, I told him my story.

Then he asked the carriage driver to tell him exactly what had happened. He did. Both stories were exactly the same, except that one was conveyed in English and one was recited in Arabic. Had our stories not been the same then it would have been necessary to ask a third party for his version. Omran struggled to contain his amusement and keep a serious face.

After hearing the facts and knowing there was no obvious solution, Omran looked me in the eye, shook his finger at me, and in an exaggerated and very authoritative stern manner (which I had never heard before) he commanded, "Go home NOW!" I was never so thankful to be ordered about and it didn't take me two seconds to go into action. I wanted out of there!

I hurried directly home, but I was still too scared to turn on the light in our apartment, thinking somebody may have followed me to learn where I lived.

So I sat in the dark, trembling, for more than an hour, and repeating over and over, my favorite Arabic phrase, "*Il hamdu lil Allah*" or Thanks be to God—and this time, thanks to Omran. From that time, whenever I encountered a carriage on the town's busy streets, the driver called out his "hello" to me and in an exaggerated manner, using hand gestures, he showed me how healthy and well-fed his horse was. Egyptians do like to tease.

Underground Belly Dancing

O mran took me to one of his favorite places: an underground belly dancing bar, which happens to be on the rooftop of a local hotel in Luxor. We had been to this place previously, but not at this hour. The party really gets going sometime after two a.m. I was the only woman (other than dancers and waitresses) in the room full of a hundred fifty men and the only non-Egyptian.

The best dancers are saved till this hour and the men want action. The audience men get up on the stage and solo dance or they dance with other men (no, this has nothing to do with sexual orientation), and in a few instances, they dance with the professional dancer.

The sensuous manner of the dancing men has always been a turn-on for me. The dancing women are curvaceous and well endowed. The dancing men are hardened and tanned with well-developed muscles.

When a dancing woman shimmies or ripples the muscles in her buttocks, it is very sexy. But when a man shimmies or ripples the same, the muscle movement is much more pronounced. I guess it's just natural for me to enjoy watching the dance moves of the men more than the moves of the women.

The woman on stage is clothed in a typical belly dancing costume, which is quite revealing for this culture. A law in Egypt says the dancing woman cannot wear a two-piece costume; her midriff must be covered. So the top and the bottom of her dancing gear are joined with an extremely sheer net-like fabric, invisible to the naked eye. But she is following the law! Her midriff is covered.

The men are clothed in their regular western street clothes, or in the traditional garment of the Egyptian male, the *galabaya*. This does not hinder my seeing and enjoying the strong muscle movement under all that fabric.

Then the money starts flying—literally. The dancing men, as well as spectators, begin throwing large bills to the dancers. Or they go onto the stage and lay a pile of bills on the head of the dancers. Of course, the money falls to the floor with the dancer's first movement and there is a special young man whose only job is to run around and gather up the money, which is later divided amongst the musicians and dancers.

We had a front row table so I could see the denominations of the bills, and I can swear that thousands of Egyptian pounds flew before my eyes.

A Rat in My Flat

Since early childhood I've had a serious phobia of mice. Intellectually I know that a mouse in my territory will do me no harm, and of course, the mouse is more frightened than I. At the sight of a mouse I get throw-up sick and break into a sweat that leaves water drops on the floor and totally soaked clothing on me.

So when I learned that I was sharing my apartment with a rat, I wasted no time running screaming to my nearest neighbor. "What shall I do?"

She screamed back, "Kill it!"

"How?" I gasped.

"With a stick!" she yelled. She could see my panic and the water dripping off my face.

Being the good neighbor that she was, she called down from her balcony to the boys playing in the street. Rushing to my rescue with big sticks, they set about cornering the animal in the kitchen, blocking the doorway so it couldn't escape, and began beating it to death; blood was squirting in every direction. During this trauma I was standing on top of the table in the dining room, my wobbly knees causing my entire body to shake, crying my heart out, and holding my hand over my mouth trying not to throw up!

Then the boys discovered that under my kitchen sink there was a nest and it was full of babies, which also had to be killed. Another rat had already escaped down the hole beside the drain pipe. I'll spare my readers the rest of the gory details. But trust me; it was completely traumatic. Hearing the bones breaking and listening to the babies crying out in pain was much too much trauma for me!

As for the neighbor boys, they gallantly cleaned up the mess in my kitchen, washed the blood and guts and rat hair from the walls and floor, mixed up some plaster and filled the unnecessary opening around the drain pipe, and bade me farewell with smiling faces.

In the desert house we rented, I investigated the noises I continually heard coming from the kitchen. It sounded like someone was in there. I discovered that someone was in there: at least one big rat. After several days of listening to noises and trying to figure out exactly where they were coming from, I determined that these animals were coming in through my open kitchen window. Well, that was easy enough to fix. I stood in the doorway, beating on a metal pot and yelling until I was sure all rats had departed through the window. I closed the window, nailed it shut and my problem was solved.

Strangely, I am more afraid of a mouse than I am of a rat but I don't want to share my home with either.

Menu in English

I am entertained from time to time by the way English is used incorrectly and that shows itself often in restaurant menus. Even though the menu often provides me with a silent laugh, I always can figure out what is meant or what is being described.

Recently Omran and I stopped at a newly opened restaurant and upon receiving the menu in English, I was shocked to discover that I absolutely could not interpret or figure out the descriptions of the foods that were printed in my own language. The menu items went like this:

- Drink Chicken

- 1 Bath Stuffed Frick

- 1 Bath Grilled

- 1 Kebab Resolved

- Evacuated Chicken

- Paper Meat

Rather than risk ordering something I wouldn't want, I settled for a salad. But I did speak to the owner and offered to make the proper corrections. He was totally uninterested. Whoever wrote the menu had used the language translation feature on the computer and he was 100% convinced that he was 100% correct.

Marriage, Sex Education, Family Expectations

Marriage is the most important event in a girl's life. Many girls become engaged at the early age of ten or eleven years. In this situation the engagement is arranged by the family and parents and the youngster may not actually become married until she reaches the legal age, recently raised to eighteen years for males and sixteen years for females. I know two elderly women who actually were married at age eleven.

In the villages of Upper Egypt, often the entire adult male family must approve an engagement before it can take place. In a family close to me, a suitor asked the parent for permission to become engaged to one of the daughters. His credentials were very good, his family history was unblemished, and he offered an excellent dowry; he seemed like the perfect match and the daughter wanted to marry this man.

Everyone in the family was in favor of this union—everyone except one half-brother who lives and works far from Luxor. He never met the suitor, never spoke with him, never talked with the half-sister, and all his information came from other male family members. I do not know the reason why, but he would not give his permission for this union to take place; therefore the engagement *did not* happen. To me, his reasons sounded weak and feeble, even for this culture. But he is the oldest and in charge of the family. Here in Upper Egypt, one does not go against the family or the responsible male.

On another occasion, I was a houseguest in the home of a girlfriend in another Egyptian village when she received a phone call from her brother in the delta region of the country. A very nice man had previously asked if she would join him in marriage and she was ready to accept his proposal. But first she needed the permission of her eldest brother, who lives many hours away but who is responsible for his sisters. Her suitor phoned the brother and presented his excellent credentials.

My girlfriend is no child—she is now in her early fifties and has never married, but the brother refused. The family is Nubian and her brother would not give her permission to marry a non-Nubian. When the brother presented this decision to the family back home, the mother wept in sorrow. My girlfriend became teary-eyed, but quickly declared, "My brother knows what is best for me," wiped away the tears and accepted his decision without further discussion. My friend's chances of ever marrying are pretty slim, I think.

It works the other way also. One of my closest friends, Riham, had been confiding in me for weeks that she did not want to marry her fiancée Rajab, who is also her first cousin. When she let some of the family in on her secret, the news did not go over well and she was forbidden to talk about it again. Well, Riham didn't talk to the family about it again, but she sure let me know her feelings and why she felt as she did. She was very torn between her own desires and her family obligations. I feared she would have a nervous breakdown. She felt that I was the only person to whom she could speak her mind.

Finally, Riham came to me, quite downtrodden, and announced that she had determined that she *will* marry her fiancée cousin, Rajab, because it will make all the family happy. But when I asked, she confided it will not make her happy. I had been filling the role of listener and not advisor, but now I felt it was time to speak out.

Based on the closeness of our relationship, and in the most basic and elementary language I could muster, we discussed marriage in general. As our conversation continued, I described just what will be expected of her in and out of the bed and asked her if this is what she wants with cousin Rajab. I explained that if she loves her husband, all this will be beautiful and wonderful and it will feel good and that she will welcome this activity, but that if she did not love her husband, it could be most unpleasant, painful and may make her quite unhappy. Knowing her as I did, I knew full well she had no idea that *all* this is a part of marriage. I learned that she didn't even know that grown men did not still look like boy babies in diapers.

As she listened the color drained from her face and she became white as a ghost; I feared she would pass out. She excused herself and left my flat and we didn't speak again for several days. During this time I knew she was giving this her most serious attention.

I learned that when she told the family of her final decision to *not* marry Rajab, her father, in his anger, confined her to the house for a period of one year—an imprisonment, of sorts. But Riham was once again the happy young woman I knew and I had no question that I made the right decision and that she made the right decision.

An interesting side story: I traveled into and out of Egypt several times, but for a variety of reasons, six years passed before I spoke with Riham again. She was now married to a man she loved and had three beautiful children. When we reconnected, the first thing she said to me, without any reminders, was, "I didn't forget what you told me, Madame. And you were right!" I knew *exactly* what she was talking about. We never discussed this subject again.

When Riham informed me of her father's edict of confinement, I was saddened, sickened and angered, but perky Riham said, "Madame, I want you to go out to all the dancers on the tourist cruise ships and in the tourist clubs and tell them what happened. Then tell them that I have much time to do their sewing and to bring their costumes to me."

I followed her instructions and then I joined my friend and the dancers as we met at Riham's home several times a week. We sat in a circle around the reception room, eagerly drinking our Egyptian tea, giggling and laughing hysterically as we recited our stories and demonstrated some of our silly and humorous experiences. If he had planned it for a month, Riham's dad could not have provided us with a more fantastic party-time.

Most marriages are business, although there are a few incidences where the bride and groom have a love match. The common belief is that a marriage based on love is doomed from the beginning. A marriage between two cousins (usually first cousins) is considered the very best and absolutely ideal. Both sides have support from the family because both sides are protecting the family honor. Neither side needs to worry that the other side has hidden secrets.

Personal desires are usually put aside for *what is best for the family*. The unity of the family is one of the reasons why village weddings are so much fun. There is no *her* side and *his* side. Literally, at the wedding everyone knows everyone and is probably related to everyone.

Likewise, if the young couple has issues that are creating problems, a counsel of family members may be called to discuss these issues, and like a jury, reach a decision about the handling of the problem. The couple having the problem is then expected to follow these recommendations.

If a young unmarried woman eyes a village man and develops feelings for him, she can do nothing but wait and hope he notices her in the same way. He can send one of the family women to inquire about her, but she cannot do the same. If any female in past generations has brought dishonor upon the family, or has caused talk or raised eyebrows, future young women from that family would be disqualified as a potential wife.

Men choose a wife based on her goodness and purity—and the goodness of her female family. I have heard it said that the honor of the family is held between the legs of the women.

She chooses a husband based on his family background, including wealth, how much gold he is willing to give her, and what kind of house or flat he will provide. Does he own land or will he inherit? He pays nearly all expenses for the wedding and pays for everything for the rest of his life. She and her family usually provide the bedroom furniture and the kitchen items. But he may be required to provide her wedding wardrobe.

The day before the wedding there is a great procession of cars with honking horns, trucks and motorcycles, singing, clapping and *ululating* women as the couple move their belongings into their new dwelling. Friends and family ooh and aah over every piece, every new set of sheets, every new dish and even every piece of her trousseau. The refrigerator and cupboards are stocked with all the necessary food stuffs.

Oftentimes the bride and groom live in his family home, blending with the family. More often, the groom builds another level on top of his family home, so the newlyweds occupy the second or third floor of the house. As sons marry, the family house grows taller. If one must live with ones in-laws, perhaps it is best if those in-laws *are* close aunts or uncles or cousins.

A young friend of mine is a very pretty girl and the older of two sisters. This young woman had dreams of becoming a doctor and was checking into colleges. Both her mother and father are illiterate. The father is very successful in business and very up-to-date on most matters, though he cannot read the names and numbers in his cell phone. The mother is very oriented toward village and family tradition. It was the mother who could not accept her daughter's dreams and ambitions and stopped any plans for her daughter becoming a doctor.

So the daughter chose a second career which was also vetoed by the mother. In the meantime, a suitor called upon the family with a request to marry this daughter's younger sister. That sister was in favor of the match, but again Mother said "no." It is tradition—and almost an unwritten law—that the older sister be married before the younger sister, so the younger one was required to turn this prospect down and hope for the best when another young man came to call—but after the older sister was married.

Now the pressure was on. The older sister had to be married so that the younger sister could then be married. That meant forgetting all desire for further education. In a relatively short time a very appropriate suitor asked for her hand in marriage and the couple married and now have children. From all appearances I would not classify this marriage as the happiest I've seen. The younger sister is now engaged to a fine man and soon to be married.

To be an unmarried woman is heartbreaking and humiliating. She must have a husband to take care of her—and children for her golden years. An unmarried woman has no status and no freedom. She always must seek permission and give an accounting to her father or brother—or other male family member. The subject of being a bride is constant on a girl's mind and she fantasizes about this time during all her growing up years. Her fantasies have nothing to do with the actual marriage and the future life together. Most of her fantasies are about this one opportunity in her life to dress in the special fancy rented dress and to visit the coiffure and to have her face elaborately made up.

One sixteen-year-old friend came running to me announcing that she is going to become engaged (family decision) sometime in the near future. Then she launched into a detailed description of how she wants her hair done and the style of dress she wants. She was very excited about the make-up she would be wearing. Then a promise was extracted from me to bring my camera to the coiffure and take lots of photos. After I had listened politely for a length of time, I inquired "Who is this lucky man?" She told me his name but without passion or excitement of voice and she told me no more about him. I don't even know if he is handsome. It's just not as important as the dress and make-up and the memories this special day will bring. Marriage is business.

Some of the very traits that may make a woman attractive and desirable in Cairo are the same traits that make it difficult to marry here in Upper Egypt. One is a university education. Many men fear having a wife who is more educated than they. Another is being employed or involved in business. So unmarried young women simply sit at home waiting for someone to come and inquire about them. To be as invisible as possible brings the most potential husbands.

If a young woman were seen publicly talking or laughing (heaven forbid!) with a young single man, she has possibly ruined her chances of ever being chosen for a bride. This activity will label her as an out of control, loose woman, suspected of no longer being a virgin. In fact, this is reason for the girl's father or older brother to kill her for bringing dishonor to the family. This subject is not talked about freely in Egypt but it still happens, though perhaps not as frequently as in the more conservative countries. In 1995 the Egyptian government reported fifty-two honor killings for that year—that's one per week—yet the majority are never reported or they are falsely reported as accidents.

When a young couple marries here in Upper Egypt, they quite possibly have never had a private conversation between the two of them, never held hands, and of course, never kissed. This might partially explain why so many brides look terrified during their wedding. Proof of her virginity must be provided as soon as possible after she and her husband are alone, and if she is so scared that she will not cooperate, her mother is called in to encourage her, or to forcibly hold her legs apart, whichever is necessary. Sometimes the bride is so scared that she *wants* her mother to be with her. On rare occasion it is necessary for three or more female relatives of the bride to sit on her and hold her down while the husband, with one of his fingers wrapped in gauze, enters her and breaks her hymen. Thus, the bloody proof of her virginity can now be shown to all.

If the new bride is extremely frightened on her wedding night and puts up resistance, some grooms think this means they need to *rough her up* a bit and take her virginity without her cooperation. He should show the bloody cloth from his conquest to prove that he is a man. On occasion, a man might suffer from anxiety and be unable to function enough to get the bloody cloth out for examination. A few men, I have heard, received their sex education by watching the farm animals in the fields and are unaware there is another way.

It is an accepted fact that unmarried Egyptian women are ignorant of sexual matters—they believe that's the way it should be. The young woman would be in very deep trouble if she were not. So it would not benefit anyone if she asked questions and had even a little understanding of what a "good lover" should be.

Young men are often just as frightened as young women. Unmarried men here do not talk about these things, not even to other men, and certainly never could they talk with their own family women about this subject. Yet they consider matters of sex and the body very natural and, when allowed to, speak without embarrassment.

You see, it *is* possible, if a young man has a good friend from the western world, to ask questions of that friend—male or female. Upper Egypt, being a place that thrives on old wives tales, has more misconceptions than truths. I've spent many hours over many cups of tea, answering questions from men friends that twelve year olds in the west might answer.

Men, here in Egypt, have very different expectations from western women and Egyptian women. They do not expect the western female to be a virgin and they do not expect her to be ignorant about sexual matters—in fact, just the opposite. I have known a number of males who did not want to save their virginity for their wedding night.

A young male friend, probably about thirty years of age, without embarrassment, asked me if I would teach him about sex. I asked him specifically what did he have in mind. His response was something like this: "Someday my family will find a bride for me and I need to know what to do when I am married. I will be embarrassed if I know nothing or if I do it wrong. I'd like for you to teach me how to have sex." Now it was pretty clear to me exactly what he had in mind. I did not find this request insulting and I certainly did not find it flattering. He just felt that a few lessons before the event would be helpful. I explained that it is good if he and his bride learn together; that he is not expected to know everything the first night—nor is she.

Sexual knowledge and education has been so lacking here that the men commonly ask me, "I know there are three places where I can put it, but I am afraid I'll put it in the wrong place and kill her. How can I know where to put it?" This is another of the old wives tales. They have had no opportunity to experiment with these ideas and to benefit from their exploration.

I have faith that computers and cellular phones, with all their pornographic movies and other explicit pictures, will help to educate these individuals. On the other hand, many porn movies present such an exaggeration; it could create another set of problems.

With this modern assistance, young women and men are learning more about life and about themselves and much of what I've mentioned above need not be the frightening experience that it has been in the past. At least, a couple can figure out how to speak together privately using the cellular phone.

It's sad to report that in recent years the divorce rate has climbed dramatically. Divorce is no longer the social stigma that it once was, and Cairo newspapers report that one third of couples separate in the first year and that one-half split in the first four years. Egypt has the highest divorce rate in the Arab world.

Village Weddings

Village weddings are all the same, yet totally different. In Upper Egypt all are held outdoors in the street or alleyway near the family home. Benches from inside the near-by homes are carried into the street for guests to sit. Music can be provided by a hired disk jockey or by live musicians and a singer.

At some weddings, everyone dances. At other times, only the younger men get in the dancing circle and really strut their stuff and compete to see whose moves are better. If there were no musical instruments except for the drums, the dancing would still go on. I have seen both the women and the men pick up a metal serving tray, or a plastic dishpan, and start beating out a rhythm and the dancing begins. After all, we *are* in Africa and the natural rhythm of southern Egypt has a distinct African feel.

There are special times when some of the older men perform the stick dance, a slow, graceful and elegant dance, almost ballet-like, where the performer impersonates a warrior. Some of the younger generations of men have added street dancing and hip-hop to their traditional moves. Weddings are a wonderful place for little boys and the little girls who have just discovered their hips, to display their ability, and they are encouraged to do so. This is also the place where young and single women, dressed to the nines, can be seen by the young and single men and their families, yet these young women must remember to display shyness in public.

But those that I most enjoy watching as they dance are the older women, who have not forgotten how to move those body parts that are kept covered by layers upon layers of black polyester fabric. By the time a woman has reached the respected *older* status, she has probably added more than a few pounds around her waist and fanny. This is all the better to perform at weddings and family parties. Despite the women being barefoot, their dances are sophisticated and elegant. Women dance alone or with women, and men dance solo or with men.

In some regions, or in some families, the men and women are segregated for the wedding celebration. Now, this is the place to see some *real* Egyptian dancing. When the women are alone, with no men to see their moves, they let go of their modesty and reserve, and the passion and soul of the woman is expressed through her dance movements. These women really give it their all.

The first time I attended this type of party, my husband escorted me to the party site. When he rang the doorbell, I could tell that someone was looking out through the "peek hole." The door opened just enough for a strong lady's arm to reach out, grasp my arm very firmly, and pull me through the small passage and into the room. I wondered when I would ever see my husband again.

I decided to be a wallflower and simply observe all the action—until one woman spoke to me in a firm voice, "Get your feet off the floor. You dance, Sister!" So I danced! After what seemed like just a short time, I was having so much fun that I really didn't think about my husband again until someone told me he was at the door and I must leave the party and go with him. I wasn't ready to leave. I had never before been given permission to be so free on the dance floor! I had never before *wanted* to give my body such freedom of movement. I surprised myself and I loved it! I felt very liberated.

As much as I like to watch the men dance, if I could choose which celebration I wish to attend, I'd choose to be segregated with the women. Still, I wish I could be a fly on the wall and see what goes on in the men's section. I bet the women have more fun!

More Village Weddings

I love going to the weddings in the villages. It seems there is a village wedding every week, but during the summer there is an abundance of them. They are simple by western standards, but not simple to the residents here. Before the wedding takes place, the legal papers have been signed by the groom and the father of the bride, thus the couple is legally married. However, the marriage cannot be consummated until the couples' intention is announced to everyone they know, via the wedding party, simply known as "the wedding" or a "village wedding." The time gap between the legalities and the wedding itself could be a matter of months.

As soon after the signing of the contract and as soon as the groom has accumulated enough money to build or complete the couples' home, then the party can be planned. Local musicians are engaged and invitations are issued via word-of-mouth—though invitations are never necessary for attendance—and the preparations begin.

The wedding activities mentioned here are standard for the smaller villages in the Luxor region of Upper Egypt. They will vary somewhat in other areas of Egypt.

Because of changing times, cultural changes are becoming necessary for village weddings. It is not so common these days for a wedding to be celebrated for four days and nights. Almost no one can afford this many days of partying and feasting. The cost of slaughtering a cow or even a sheep, makes feeding the entire family, friends and neighbors prohibitive.

But one custom that continues is *El Layla el Henna* (the Night of the Henna), always the evening before the wedding. These days this custom is reserved for the bride only but in times past the groom and his friends also received henna. Usually henna is applied to the arms, hands, feet, and sometimes to the lower legs. For a wedding, henna designs may be applied to more personal and private areas of the body. This too is a loud event—anytime women gather to celebrate, there is much ululating.

While live music loudly fills the village, the bride and her friends all gather in the bride's family home and the local henna artist paints elaborate designs on the arms and feet of the bride. Other guests receive henna also, but theirs is much less elaborate—somewhat of a token. This is definitely a beautification ritual. Some of the guests simply have the palms of their hands dyed the orange—red—brown of the henna. This will stay on the skin for a week to ten days.

Typically the bride wears a white western style wedding dress, which is covered with lace, feathers, ruffles, rhinestones, pearls, sequins, and any other glittery materials that can possibly be applied. She has been to the coiffure and, for the only time in her life, she is wearing elaborate make-up and an elaborate hair style. She may be without *hijab* (hair covering) or she may have a very elaborate *hijab*. This is her choice but it is perfectly acceptable to uncover her hair on this night.

There seems to be a standard bridal hair-do and make-up, as most brides have a cookie cutter appearance and most, I think, are nearly unrecognizable for all the heavy make-up and painted features on faces that are usually scrubbed clean. On the eve of the wedding, she, along with her friends, goes to visit the coiffure; the bride dressed in her white wedding dress. Sitting through the three hour, or longer, procedure in the wedding dress simply can't be comfortable.

Her make-up is applied in the coiffure's shop and I'm sure all make-up comes from the same bottle, including the very heavily applied, silvery sky blue sparkle eye make-up. The pancake makeup on her face is several shades too light for her skin color and therefore, she has a ghostly appearance. Her hair has had streaks bleached into it with tendrils hanging in front of her face. She probably has had false fingernails applied and brightly polished. Her arms and other exposed body parts are displaying the henna from the night before. To the bride, her family and friends, she looks exquisitely beautiful and that is what every bride in the world wants to achieve.

The groom and his buddies crowd into rented or borrowed vans and cars, led by a motorcycle brigade, to go to the coiffure shop and pick up the bride. Most couples at this point go to the photo shop—which is often wisely located beside the coiffure—and have this event memorialized in photos. The bride and groom and their friends then go to their wedding party, where the village people await their arrival.

With the bride and groom secured in the back seat of a car, and all the friends and family crammed into cars and vans or on motorcycles, the party now forms a parade, driving wildly and madly around the town or villages, all horns blaring constantly, the women *ululating*, the others clapping and shouting.

Visitors to Egypt have probably seen a parade of fifteen or so cars and motorcycles going through the village or town with horns blaring, music blasting, women ululating, people hanging from car and van windows while others stand on the top of the moving vehicle and dance. They appear insane from every angle: erratic and crazy driving, tailgating, passing on the wrong side, driving on the wrong side, cars and motorcycles weaving in and out—anything you can think of that is wrong and insane, they are doing it.

Well, I rode in one of these wedding processions. Not only was I in the car, but Omran was driving it. I was so scared that I cried all the way and I was sure I would vomit all over everyone, but fortunately I didn't. We even drove down the railroad tracks, straddling the rails! I did NOT enjoy any of that at all and, rest assured, my first time is my last time. It is one of the most unsafe, barbaric and stupid things I have ever witnessed—or been a part of. But they think it is wonderful fun. Sometimes serious accidents do happen.

Three Weddings

Three weddings in one were a bit much, but these were family weddings and they were in close proximity to each other—all in the same village. It becomes confusing to me, trying to keep everyone in the family connected. When I hear something like "She's my cousin: her sister married my mother's cousin's brother-in-law," I marvel. I wouldn't exactly consider this a cousin, but here they often stretch the boundaries. There is nothing more important than *family* and most villagers will do anything for family. Generosity reigns here on the west bank.

A village wedding is nothing more than a big party to acknowledge and celebrate a couple's legal and religious union. There is no ceremony at this event, no vows said, nor invitations sent, no food or drink or gifts given, but it is safe to say that "a good time is had by all." It's the perfect time to socialize with family and friends and to dance the night away.

There was a wedding that Omran particularly wanted to be a part of. The young groom is a waiter at the local coffee house, so he is well acquainted with all the men in the surrounding villages. I'm told that he has a "terrible family." I didn't press for details, but I noticed that no person in his immediate family attended the wedding. This is highly unusual.

The young man had no savings, and had no hopes for a marriage. Never-the-less, he fell in love with a lovely girl from Omran's village (yes, a relative of Omran's) and they shared dreams of marriage, even though believing it could never happen.

A patron of the coffee shop learned of this and secretly gave the young man a few hundred Egyptian pounds, hoping he might be able to rent a small flat and move in with his bride after merely signing the marriage papers. I learned very early on that here on the west bank of Luxor, one does nothing secretly. The news of the patron's silent generosity spread like wildfire and then *everyone* wanted to take action.

Someone paid for the musicians, another paid for the bride's dress, two months' rent on the flat was donated, the coiffure for the bride was donated, and another person stocked the refrigerator with food. I am sure that someone from every household in three villages attended this wedding. I do believe that the guests outnumbered those attending our wedding.

Omran's contribution was to finance one of the cars used in that parade of crazy and barbaric driving. No, I did not participate in that portion of the wedding. But, in general, this wedding was one of the happiest weddings I've been to.

Younger Men, Older Women

Here in Upper Egypt there is a totally new social aspect occurring and becoming rather common: marriage between Egyptian men and western women; namely between *younger* Egyptian men and *older* western women. This is especially common here in the tourist center of Luxor. Through their work with tourists a great many men have an opportunity to meet and socialize with western women. Many men use this opportunity to practice their language skills and to learn an off-the-job vocabulary. The western woman loves the attention she receives from the young handsome men and returns to her home country raving about her holiday romance, thus more women come solo to Egypt each year. The inevitable happens and couples do fall in love.

In recent years the west bank of Luxor economy has grown phenomenally with much of the money for commercial buildings, homes and other types of business coming from the new western wife and the young Egyptian husband. Both can be winners. In Egypt her currency will buy more than it will in her home country, and her partner husband provides his language and cultural expertise, which she desperately needs to be a business woman, while he learns new skills.

Living in a very poor country, this young husband could never earn enough to invest in a business in his own country. For the Upper Egyptian man there is no other way to get out of the rut he is in and to get ahead. He knows that marriage to a western woman—one with money—provides his only way out.

Now that so many western women have provided the funding for hotels, restaurants, and the like, the landscape has been enhanced and beautified, jobs for locals have been provided, business education is available and the owners reap their own great rewards of success. Most of these marriages prove successful to varying degrees, although there are enough horror stories to make one leery of taking that first step.

It is acceptable in Islam for a man to marry a Christian or Jewish woman. But an Islamic woman cannot marry a man other than Muslim. When the Egyptian Islamic man is attracted to a western woman, he wants to marry her, as marriage is the only thing he knows. His religion is adamant about no sex outside of marriage, and the law also forbids it. An Egyptian man cannot walk in the street with a western woman of his choice unless he has certain papers identifying him as one who works with tourists—or is married to a tourist. These are not given freely. Without this he could be jailed—at least in Upper Egypt.

But, the Egyptian government makes it very easy for the female tourist and the Egyptian man. To prevent the man from committing the grave sin of sex without marriage, he and his woman can visit an attorney's office and fill out a paper and pay a big sum of money and they now have an *Orfi* marriage. This is no more than permission from the government to have sex and to share an apartment. This does not allow the couple to stay in a hotel together without police interference. Another paper is necessary for that—at a higher cost. These papers are absolutely worthless for anything else. The wife has no rights, nor does her spouse.

The paper can be torn up at any time and the "marriage" is finished. To be legally married, a couple must travel to the government offices in Cairo. I have heard of Egyptian men who have had dozens of *Orfi* marriages, each lasting overnight to a couple of weeks, and I have heard of vacationing western women who come to Egypt without their legitimate husbands because they have *Orfi* marriages here. For many of the couples this is not serious business. It often keeps the western woman returning to Egypt for her holidays and the Egyptian man is happy to be entertained while she is in town for a week or two. Most of us in the west would call this having an affair.

A Muslim man can have up to four legitimate wives at the same time. Many men with an *Orfi* marriage to a western woman also have a legitimate Muslim marriage and family with a fellow Egyptian. Here in Upper Egypt that marriage is usually with a cousin and was probably arranged by the family.

Children

My, oh my! There are lots of children! Most Egyptians still produce big families, even though the government encourages birth control and makes it easily available. A woman's value and worth, in many cases, is determined by the number of children she produces, particularly the number of sons. Also, if a woman gives her husband many children (she believes), he will not want another wife, a philosophy I fail to completely understand.

Egypt's population is growing extremely fast and agricultural land is shrinking as arable land must be used for housing. The religion encourages large families and agricultural activity encourages large families

Even though there is more celebrating when a boy child comes into this world, girls are welcomed, treasured, coddled, and adored. All children are lovingly looked after by all adults. It warms my heart to watch the interaction between aunts and uncles and the children of the family. Rarely does an adult encounter a child without giving a spontaneous gift. That gift is usually a small amount of money, which is spent immediately on a little bag of potato chips, here called *"chibsee"*. But in recent times, I've noticed that when a little boy gets fifty *piasters* (less than ten cents) he runs off to the internet café to play games.

Once tiny children get past that shy stage, they become very outgoing and it seems to me that they lose their childhood early. I think they "grow up" very fast. Maybe they need to—a lot is expected of them. I am frequently escorted and protected by a five year old boy. Children here appear less dependent on their parents.

I've watched children playing in situations I consider very dangerous, but the loving parents seem not to be disturbed. Children run in the streets with the multitudes of vehicles, darting in and out. They play with butcher knives and other items that I would never allow my own to play with. There are no curfews or predetermined bedtimes. There's nothing unusual about six year olds playing in the street at one or two o'clock in the morning. Maybe this prepares them for life's challenges later on. Children, especially boys, receive very little—if any—discipline, yet most grow up to become very responsible, caring, giving, honest, and moral individuals.

Many children begin working in the family business at a very early age. If papa owns a fruit and vegetable stand, there's a lot a youngster can do there. At the same time, he is learning the family business. I've witnessed children under the age of twelve *operating* the family business in two or three languages—and with the ability to get the correct language with each new tourist face. I am totally amazed at the ability with numbers this experience has given these kids, yet they can't identify Egypt on a map and possibly can't read their own language.

When I'm on the street, elementary school-age children flock around me because they want to practice the English they are learning in school. Often, it is limited to "Hello. What's your name?" Sometimes they just call out to me "Good morning teacher" without understanding what they are really saying. Yesterday a little boy added "How old are you?" in very elementary English. I responded in the same style English, "I am ten years old." It was an acceptable answer—probably better than if I had told the truth. He would not have understood a higher number in English.

Sometimes when the children are calling out to me, I don't pay much attention. But a group of very young boys got my attention when I heard them yelling "Good morning sexy lady!" After checking to see if there were other women in the vicinity, I smiled to myself and walked on, knowing they had no idea what they were saying.

Along with all this goodness, there is a negative side. Somewhere in their young lives, a small number of children have learned to say things to tourists like "Hello. Give me *bakshish* (money)." This presents a very bad image and it is not encouraged. Again, I doubt these youngsters truly understand what they are saying.

Islamic Names

I slamic names are amazingly easy to understand, once you know the secret.

Each new born is given one name; let us say it is Ahmed. Always his second name is the given name of his father; let us say it is Ali. Therefore, all brothers and sisters have the same second name. His third name is the given name of his grandfather; let us say it is Khalil. This could be carried out to six or seven generations, but for most, three is sufficient. This newborn's name is Ahmed Ali Khalil.

When Ahmed Ali Khalil has a child, that child's name will be placed first and all the other names will be moved over, with the last one being dropped. So, one's entire family lineage is right there in the name.

The same applies to girl's names. If Ahmed had a sister with the given name of Mona, she would be Mona Ali Khalil.

I know a man whose name is Mohamed Mohamed Mohamed. I think no one is apt to forget his name. If your family followed this naming practice, what would you call yourself?

Walk Like an Egyptian

Life was slow and simple. For me to have an enriching experience in Egypt meant that, as much as possible, I needed to live like an Egyptian, think like an Egyptian, act like an Egyptian and embrace their culture wholeheartedly. This was not an intellectual decision, but rather one that came from deep within, more like a burning desire. It came from my gut. I was in the place that I called home and I very much felt like I belonged.

Over the years I've known a few western women who lived in the Luxor area and most were married to Egyptian men. Rarely were these women accepted into the Egyptian family in the warm and welcoming way that I was. Often I've been asked, "Why?" My response has always been short and sweet: because I know the rules and I follow them. But it goes deeper than that. You see, I *was* home when I was with the family. My Egyptian friends felt that also and they gave me the Egyptian name Fatma and referred to me as "sister" or "auntie."

Egyptians like having western friends and welcome them into their lives, but the western women have the responsibility of knowing the rules of the culture and religion and following them. Some western women just don't want to invest time into doing that. If only they understood the richness of the life they are missing. Even in the 115 degree heat the Egyptian women would be embarrassed to take me to visit their family home if I appeared in a low-cut sleeveless dress that hit me above the knees. In their eyes I would look like a prostitute. If I spent too much time being friendly with the men of the family, I would never be invited again. I pleased the elderly of the family by giving the show-of-respect-kiss on the back of the hand. Even having a hijab on my head made a world of difference in the way I was accepted and treated. To carry out my desires was not difficult. In fact, it was extremely easy for me. It felt perfectly natural and I embraced it fully.

The life of an Egyptian revolves around the family. They cannot envision a person without such, so I was included in many different family events. I am told that in the Arabic language there are two separate words meaning alone. One word *wahid* (alone) means being without company momentarily. The other word *yatim* (orphan) is so seldom used that most people don't even know it.

Years prior to living in Egypt, I hosted a dinner party in my home where the conversation turned to whether we American women should cover our hair when visiting in a country where covering is traditional. The eight women in attendance were equally divided. Half of us felt that for an American to cover her hair was a mockery, as it was not a part of *our* religious beliefs. One woman suggested that this would be an insult to Islam and to the women of the host country. The other half of us felt that to cover our hair would be just the opposite—a sign of respect for the religion and culture. I was part of the latter group and carrying out my belief has opened many doors to new friendships, invitations and new cultural experiences.

Many of my women friends told me how much they appreciated my wearing the *hijab*. Many asked me why I covered. My response was simple, "Out of respect." This pleased them immensely. I have a closet which overflows with colorful and beautiful scarves, all gifts from Egyptian women friends.

Covering my hair was a bit like going under cover, quite literally. Since many people couldn't determine if I was Egyptian or tourist, I was rarely hassled by the annoyances in the street that drive tourists mad. It also enabled me to pay Egyptian prices with less hassle.

One evening as I walked along a Luxor street, I heard a loud male voice, speaking accented English, coming directly from behind me. It was obvious his comment was directed at me. "Thank you for respecting our women and our traditions," he called out. An Egyptian woman would not have acknowledged the man, but I could not stop myself. I turned and with a smile, I told him it gives me much pleasure to do so.

One sweet friend, Amal, was fascinated with my clothing. Everything came from America, but I wore it all in the style of Egypt. My blouses were not tight across my bosom and they all had long sleeves and high necklines. My skirts were an inch or two above the floor, as was popular. Styles change somewhat from region to region in Egypt, but that was easy to deal with.

I sometimes stayed with Amal's family for a week at a time. Every morning, she went through my suitcase and admired or rejected each article of clothing. "Very good, Madame Jonna." Or she clicked her tongue in a way that, in Egypt, means "no" then she laid out what she thought I should wear that day.

She often put things together in a combination I would never choose, but I always wore what she decided. She herself was smartly dressed and this was a good way for me to learn. My objective was to blend in and be a part of the culture.

Around the house, women wear a *galabaya*, a loose fitting full length, long sleeved dress that reminded me of a granny nightgown. Now-a-days, inside and out of sight, upper class women might even wear jeans or tights. But no outsider would ever enter her home until she donned her *galabaya* or *abaya* over the casual wear.

In summer the *galabaya* is made of a lightweight cotton or polyester. In winter it is made of heavier fabric, often what we in the west call polyester fleece. Polyester is a very popular fabric in the Middle East. They often confuse fine polyester with silk. The Egyptian women seem to like the durability of polyester and the fact that it holds the color well and doesn't need to be ironed. When I tried to talk about polyester being too hot in summer, I could find no one to agree with me.

Outside their homes, the women are always clothed in an *abaya* which is a plain black, long sleeve, full length, high neck, full cut garment that is worn over other clothing, no matter the weather. Under her *abaya* she could be wearing a bikini or designer jeans—though most likely she has on a simple house *galabaya*. Her head is covered with a very plain black scarf or multiple scarves so that not a hair is seen. She wears no make-up but she appears clean and dressed for a special occasion.

I like wearing the *abaya*. It is very much a convenience and saves a lot of time and effort. If I need or want to leave my home for a quick shopping trip, I simply put on one of my *abayas* and "toss" my scarf around my head and I am perfectly dressed and perfectly groomed, no need to even comb my hair. I've even gone into the village wearing my nightgown, covered by my *abaya*, of course. The best kept secret: many of us western women who wear the *abaya* don't always feel the need for undergarments of any sort. Talk about comfortable.

Women don't start wearing the *abaya* until they reach adulthood. Young, unmarried girls rarely wear this garment. For Egyptian women, this black cover is standard wear and you will never see her outside her home in colorful street clothes again. For me, I take advantage of both cultures and wear the *abaya* as I see fit.

Men also dress in the *galabaya* although theirs has an exclusive and distinctive design, which has not changed in many generations, if ever. It is cut in an A-line shape, with loose flowing sleeves and it falls gracefully from the shoulders to below the ankle. Most men's *galabayas* have a large hidden pocket which can carry almost as much as a woman's purse. A woman would never wear a garment cut in the style of a man's garment.

Every Egyptian man's *galabaya* is the same style, although there is a selection of half dozen or so colors in Egyptian cotton. White is the color of choice in summer. In winter, for warmth a man may wear two or more *galabayas* at the same time, as few people own coats or jackets. A more successful man wears a wool garment in winter.

It would seem that every shop in town would carry *galabayas,* but not so. I never saw a man's *galabaya* in a retail shop. They are all custom made and each man has his own favorite tailor. The length is critical. The hem must be about an inch from the ground. Even toddlers and school children wearing the *galabaya* have them custom made.

Most men wear a long scarf, wrapped as a turban around their heads. In summer, the turban is thin loosely woven white cotton and serves to protect the head from the unbearable sun. In winter, the turban is called a *shal,* often made from wool or a beautiful brocade-like woven wool and silk fabric, and it serves to keep the heat in and the cold out. Night time in the desert can be cold in winter. The *shal* is also worn wrapped around the neck and shoulders for warmth.

Some men wear western clothes during business hours, switching to the comfort of the galabaya when the workday is finished and it's time to visit the *ghawah.* Among the teenagers and younger men, western-style fashions are popular.

The long flowing *galabaya* does not hinder any activity. I have observed *galabaya*-clad men doing everything from riding horses and camels to climbing ladders during building construction, to shimmying up date palm trees to cut down the luscious fruits.

In some of my literature, I read an expression: "He ran with his tails in his teeth . . . .," but it made no sense to me at the time. The explanation was really very simple and I saw it demonstrated many times. When the *galabaya* might get in the way of some activity, such as running very fast, the men pick up the hems and pull them up to their mouth, where they hold them tight between their clinched teeth. I saw this particularly in the fields when the men were working in the irrigation ditches.

I love to watch the *galabaya* wearing men during the horse races. They are excellent horsemen and the faster they ride, the further their *galabayas* puff and flow in the wind.

What is Beauty

My Nubian friend Nadia is very beautiful. I think that Nubians have the most beautiful facial structure and features and they also have very dark skin. Some Nubians are a rich ebony color. One friend told me that she hoped she never had a daughter because she would not want another child to suffer as she had suffered because of her skin color. Indeed, once when she was visiting me in Luxor, she met with color discrimination from a vegetable vendor. When she told me about this, my American sense of fairness flared and I wanted to go and speak to the vendor, but she would not allow such a thing. You can bet your bottom dollar that I never purchased another thing from *that* vendor.

On the other hand, I am considered by many to be beautiful simply because my skin is white. As flattering as it is to be called "beautiful," I don't feel it is a valid expression because it is based solely on the whiteness of my skin. One evening I was on my way to visit a new doctor and I went into the wrong building. I asked a woman I saw in the dimly lit hall where I could find the doctor's office. She looked at me and gasped, "Oh Madame, you are very beautiful. You are very white! Please may I touch you?" She was a delightful woman, I learned as we conversed. It was like chatting with a best friend. She wanted to know all about me, and I had many questions for her.

I had an opportunity to say to this woman that I thought she was very beautiful. I verbally admired her dancing dark eyes and her full lips and the color of her skin—some of the things that made us appear different. I pointed out just how much brighter her 21 karat gold bracelets looked on her dark arm. My gold bracelets sort of fade away on my light color skin.

After she directed me to the doctor, we parted with praise and thanks to God. I remember very well that brief conversation in the nearly dark hall because it was such a warm conversation. Two women, strangers a moment ago, standing in an empty hallway, each of us sincerely admiring the beauty that we saw in the other. I think the world would be a better place for me if I had more occasions like that one. Sadly, I never saw that woman again. I know I would have enjoyed a friendship with her.

Friends in the US often ask me about the attitude of the Egyptian women toward me. They seem to think there may be some rivalry or lack of acceptance coming from them. Nothing could be further from the reality. The women of Egypt have always welcomed me with generous acceptance and assistance. They want to befriend me.

I'm always given the choice seat, the finest piece of meat, the cleanest and best of whatever is being offered. When I'm in a person's home and chicken is being cooked, the lady of the house always slyly slips the cooked chicken liver out of the pot and places it very hot into my mouth—it's a real delicacy in Egypt. It's a good thing that I like chicken liver—even though it does burn my tongue and throat.

Even before I learned any of the language, the women and I developed close relationships. I call it the language of the eyes, but I really think it is more the language of the woman's heart. Without the friendship and generosity of Egyptian women, I would not have adjusted well into this culture. They told me where to go for everything I needed, often sending one of their children to escort me, and very importantly, they informed me what I should pay, as everything here is purchased through bartering.

In the tourist areas of Egypt it is known that tourists are sold tickets for specific trains only. But I seem to have a knack for getting on the Egyptian-only, cheaper ticket trains.

Either I want to travel at a certain time or I want to go someplace where tourists don't go, such as my friend's rural village in Nubian Egypt. Usually I think it is because an Egyptian makes the ticket purchase for me.

Because my attire is proper and I can communicate in the local language, this has never been a problem. I've never met a person who wasn't eager to help me. Often times a woman with lighter skin is considered more desirable for a wife. One woman very proudly told me she was chosen first as a bride, over her sisters, and that her sisters are whiter than she. I never understood why many Egyptian people consider a person with light color skin more beautiful than a person with darker skin. They call a light skinned person "white." Proud mothers paraded their light skinned children before me to show me how white they were. One very proud mom lifted her young daughter's dress to show me her tummy, just to prove that she was white all over. Skin color is a common topic of conversation and is mentioned often.

I was engaged in a conversation on this subject with a very good Egyptian male friend. He insisted that I would be the same color as he if I spent more time out in the sun. I explained about skin pigment and even suggested that if he stayed in doors for the rest of his life, he still would be darker than I. He could not see things my way. So, in my frustration, I said, "Khalid, what color is your butt?" he thought for a moment. "Oh yes. I think you are right!" Now he understood—I think.

A Woman's Beauty

Not a lot of women in Egypt wear a covering over their face, called a *niqab*. When they do so, it's a rather short veil, beginning just below the eyes, and in recent years is an acknowledgement of their fundamentalist religious beliefs. Some of these women also wear gloves, even in the hot summer months.

Omran and I sat in the ghawah, sipping our sweet tea and going over the days' activities when one of our neighbors walked by, totally covered with just a speck of eye showing. I'm surprised I could even identify her in order to offer a greeting. At that time, it was rare in Egypt to see a woman in this style dress, so I asked my husband why she was completely covering her face. He gave my question very little thought and his answer was surprising. In Arabic he said, "If a man thinks his wife is extremely beautiful and he does not want to share that with other men, he can tell her to cover her face so that no other man can see her beauty."

Leaning forward and wiping the smile from my face, I put my hands on my hips as I stood up. "Well then, why haven't you said to me . . . . ?"

In English I heard, "Oh, oh, I know I in trouble now. I in really big trouble. I try to stop words, but words keep coming. I no want to say like that." He was quickly able to redeem himself with his lavish declarations of love and praise of my beauty and many other things that we women like to hear, in any language.

A lot of my friends in Egypt wear make-up, particularly around their eyes. Imagine a country where for thousands of years, women have adorned their eyes, lips, and cheeks with color! You see it on ancient tomb and temple walls. The people have beautiful, large, dark almond-shaped eyes, which are enhanced when outlined in black kohl.

Kohl is simply ground galena or lead sulfide and ancient women used it as protection against eye ailments. Others believed that kohl protected their eyes from the sun's rays, much as we use sunglasses today. The debate as to whether the use of kohl causes lead poisoning is ongoing. In Egypt it is often applied to the eyes of newborn babies.

I am always fascinated to watch a woman apply her kohl. She dips the slender wooden stick into the kohl pot, withdraws it when it is covered with black kohl, and places the stick against her lower eye lid. She then closes her upper eye lid against the lower area of her eye. With the kohl stick between, she smoothly draws the stick between the two lids, lining both upper and lower lid at the same time—all done to perfection without the aid of a mirror.

In the beginning, for special occasions, the women always wanted to make up my face. I think they thought that my eyes would be as beautiful as theirs if I had the same eye make-up. I often wished my eyes *could* appear as theirs, but the women in my family were blessed with deep set eyes and upper lids almost obscured. No amount of kohl would change that. When they applied liner to my eyes, it burned my eyes to tears and ran down my cheeks and smeared all over my face. It did nothing to enhance my looks and the women finally considered me hopeless and gave up. However, after my first visit home to America, I returned to Egypt with eyeliner more suitable to my eyes and I wore it for special occasions.

Women and Gold

No matter the style of dress or the region of the country, one thing is essential among the women of Egypt. Every woman, no matter her station in life, owns at least a few pieces of eighteen or twenty-one karat gold jewelry. She may have inherited it from her mother, but more likely it was a gift from her husband at the time of engagement or marriage.

Usually the father of the bride stipulates to the future groom how much gold is required for the hand of his daughter. If there is little money to be spent, a smaller amount of gold is requested. The father knows the financial status of the potential groom's family. Since few grooms have the means to make the purchase, family members usually offer him some financial assistance.

Throughout her life, the Egyptian woman desires gold. It is always a topic of conversation. Very small pieces of gold jewelry are given to newborn girls and again on their birthdays. Within days of birth, a baby girl's ears are pierced and gold rings are inserted. It felt odd when going to visit a newborn baby girl and taking jewelry for her pierced ears. I don't believe most women have ever heard of diamonds, emeralds, or pearls. Gold is the only jewelry worn. Any new piece of gold jewelry is immediately noticed and commented on by all.

Even elementary school age girls asked me about my gold and wanted to examine it. When a woman acquires a new piece of gold, everyone immediately says *mabruk*, which means congratulations. Walking through the gold bazaars of any town one sees many shops with bright shiny deep yellow gold jewelry.

Many years ago, when I decided to begin my own collection of twenty-one karat gold bracelets, I sought out the shops that usually had the largest gatherings of Egyptian women inside. I reasoned that I would find the best prices there and the best quality and workmanship. Every man, woman and child knows the daily price of a gram of twenty-one karat gold. It is announced several times each day on the radio and television. Some jewelry is made from eighteen karat, but the deeply colored twenty-one karat is the gold of desire. Egyptian women are not impressed with our pale colored western fourteen karat gold.

I had gone to a rural home, some miles from Luxor, to welcome the new-born baby of my sister-in-law. I took my camera along and before concluding the visit, I was encouraged to take a photograph of me holding the baby. Almost as an afterthought, I invited the grandmother to be in the photo. She eagerly agreed but asked me to wait a moment as she excused herself from the room.

Shortly she returned, adorned in a special gold trimmed black abaya and all her gold jewelry and sat down for the snapshot. On her hands she prominently displayed treasured and glittering gold rings. Over her head, the *hijab* was arranged so that her gold earrings were very obvious. I could feel this woman's pride and see it in her eyes. It filled the room.

Om Mustafa

S he was married at age eleven; the same age her mother had been when she became the bride of Ali. The marriage took place in her home village of Qus, a short distance from Luxor, Egypt and in this region, at this time, there was nothing unusual about marriage at such a tender age.

Indeed, her family had arranged the engagement a number of years previously, and now the family decided that the time had come. Om Mustafa was marrying one of her first cousins, somewhat older than she, a tradition in Upper Egypt. She had never attended school—it just wasn't important for a girl in that part of Egypt at that time. Therefore, she never learned to read or write or count.

Her cooking skills were praised by her family. I was fortunate to have enjoyed many delicious meals, seated with the family on her earthen floor. The western palate is accustomed to a wide variety of food, each prepared in a myriad of ways. In her home, I ate the same things during every visit: rice, tomatoes, white cheese, scrambled eggs, *baladi* bread and vegetable or salad. Like other families in the village, meat was served on special occasions only, but hopefully, most families ate it at least once a month. Yet each meal I ate in her home tasted better than the one before it.

Once a woman delivers a boy child, she is thereafter known as the mother of that son, thus Mother of Mustafa or Om Mustafa. She is part of my Egyptian family, yet I don't know her given name. Traditional and conservative women do not let their name be known. It is a highly guarded secret. Her name was whispered to me once, but it was such an unfamiliar and old-fashioned name, I quickly forgot and did not have the courage to ask for a repeat.

When her widowed mother died, with pride Om Mustafa stepped into the role of the family matriarch. Wearing the queen's crown would not have made her any more proud! Now, she did all in her power to direct the lives of her own eight children, two of their spouses, four grandchildren, her own five living brothers and their growing families. Somewhat like running a corporation, I'd say.

The first thing on her to-do list was to find a wife for the three unmarried brothers. For most of us, this would be challenge enough, but according to tradition, Om Mustafa had to find the three wives from within the family. There were no female cousins in our region, so Om Mustafa's quest took her to the distant family in Cairo, where she searched among second and third cousins, and even cousins once removed.

No one could have considered her importance any greater than Om Mustafa herself. During her search for a bride, she had to make frequent trips to Cairo, where she was treated as an honored guest by various distant relatives. They didn't know that she had sat up all night on a wooden bench, with no back, in the foul smelling third class rail car during the grueling thirteen hour train trip. With each trip to Cairo, Om Mustafa felt she was closer to her goal. Finally, at last she was successful. She found a lovely and beautiful bride for her brother, Bakr.

Exhausted from her mission and the thirteen hour ride in the hot and dirty train, she still imagined, and began planning, a big party to celebrate the approaching engagement. They would have a tent over the street, and she would help Bakr choose the engagement dress he would buy for his fiancée, there would be live music and plenty of cola for everyone. The party would go on and on and Om Mustafa would receive much praise for making such a good choice. These were Om Mustafa's ideas.

But brother Bakr had ideas of his own. While Sister was busy with her business, Bakr was busy too. Perhaps he just needed something to jump-start him into action, perhaps Sister's actions served as a wake-up call, but Bakr awakened to the realization he was very much in love with a young woman, Soha, who worked as the receptionist at the business he managed. They had known each other for several years, worked together every day, and Bakr had finally sought permission to go to her father and request that he and Soha become engaged. That permission had been granted. Now that they were engaged Bakr could call on Soha and her family and begin to plan a wedding.

Poor Om Mustafa. She was devastated! Humiliated! Angry! It was a very long time before she spoke to her brother again. I'm not sure she has spoken yet to Soha, and nobody knows just how she broke this humiliating news to the Cairo family. Secretly, the other unmarried brothers were relieved. They were now free to pursue their own search for brides and each brother already had someone in mind. Om Mustafa has not lost her prestigious position as family matriarch. Now she can add three more to her growing family—the young son and twin daughters of Bakr and Soha.

Egyptian Trust

C redit cards are totally useless here in Upper Egypt. A visit to the ATM for cash means a special trip to Luxor for me. On numerous occasions I have discovered a shortage of Egyptian pounds when I attempted to pay for my purchase. Always I suggest that the merchant hold the merchandise and I will return tomorrow with the proper funds. Instead, always the merchant says, "No Madame, you take this with you and you pay me when it is convenient for you. Don't worry." Even if I have never shopped with this merchant previously, I get the same response.

Basically, Egyptians are very honest people and they expect and assume that everyone else is also. In this situation I have never seen a merchant make a note or ask me to sign anything. He relies on his memory and I rely on mine. I would never ask for this favor, but it is generously offered.

Egyptian Hospitality—
Banana Island

Often I emphasize the Egyptian hospitality. On a very hot day we sailed in a felucca—the ancient sailing vessel which has been plying these Nile waters for thousands of years—to Banana Island, so named for the banana groves there. It's a short trip but it gives us relief from the city noises, the cars, and all the people. It feels a little cooler. There's no activity for the visitor, except to drink a cola or tea and smoke a shisha and simply to relax and watch the river flow by. That's one of the things that makes it so pleasurable.

On this afternoon my stomach was making a lot of noise, reminding me that I had not given it nourishment since yesterday noon. I inquired to one of the waiters who lived there on the island if there was any place to buy food. His response: "No Madame, but if you like Egyptian food my wife will make you something and I will bring it here."

Of course, on Banana Island I accepted and simply devoured my typical Egyptian lunch of home grown tomatoes with homemade white cheese, beans reheated from the morning meal, eggs cooked in a *tagine* (casserole), and the wonderful bread baked in Madame's mud oven, along with steaming hot tea. Oh yes, and bananas! Egypt's bananas are about half the size of most bananas and at least twice as sweet. Upon finishing such a special meal, prepared especially for me, I inquired: "How much?" The answer to my question was also very typically Egyptian: "As you like, Madame. As you like."

Summer Heat

In the hot summer months, the clock is somewhat reversed. Many shops close during the unbearable heat of the day, and people stay inside the house where they might have a ceiling fan, or possibly an air conditioner in one room. But from eleven p.m. until the wee hours of the morning, the population comes to life.

Omran and I have been going to bed around five in the morning, and then sleeping until around two-thirty the next afternoon. It's one of our ways of dealing with temperatures of 108—115. Sometimes I get quite confused because I'm not sure which meal I am eating. I suppose it doesn't matter because we eat when we are hungry. A schedule like this makes it very difficult to take medication at the proper intervals. We can't remember if we showered yesterday or an hour ago. It's a little crazy!

Speaking of heat, of course, I keep my cosmetics and toiletries in the refrigerator. I accidentally left a tube of lipstick in the bathroom for about ten minutes and when I picked it up, the lipstick poured out, all over everything. Sunscreen just slides off my face and any kind of makeup use is a joke. Even my hair gets nothing but a comb and a ponytail clip.

I learned a trick from my mother-in-law. She is swathed in black but she dips her headdress in cold water then wraps herself in it. I've learned a trick or two on my own: I wet my clean underwear under the faucet and then keep it in the refrigerator. When I put on wet, cold undies it feels good for about fifteen minutes—about the length of time it takes for my body heat to dry them. But fifteen minutes of feeling cool is a wonderful treat in the desert.

Nubia

Nubia was once a separate country located in what is now southern Egypt and northern Sudan. In pharaonic times Nubia and Egypt constantly feuded. Eventually, peace was declared and part of Nubia became a part of Egypt. The other part of Nubia became part of Sudan. This land is in one of the harshest climates in the world. The heat is unbearable and rain is non-existant.

In the 1960s Egypt set about building the Aswan High Dam and creating the huge Lake Nasser—the world's longest lake. All the magnificent temples, tombs and other buildings of antiquity, and the homes, villages and cities of the Nubians were set to be destroyed by the covering of lake water. The government of Egypt forced thousands of Nubians to flee their homeland and relocate in other areas of the country. The majority of Nubians resettled in Southern Egypt, giving this region the identity of Nubian Egypt. Nubians have maintained their own cultural identity and even continue to use their own Nubian language, as well as Egyptian Arabic.

Recently, after a visit to my girlfriend's rural Nubian Egypt village, I was a little confused about the train schedule (if, indeed there is one). At the station I spotted a group of half dozen Nubian women chatting together, so I approached them to ask about my train. They were helpful with information and they invited me to stay with them and they would be sure I got on the correct train and in the correct coach. I accepted their invitation and they kept their promise.

As we stood by the train tracks awaiting the train, I admired the dresses of the Nubian women. In this region women wear a particular style of loose sheer black lace dress over their colorful regular clothing. The lace is see-through, very pretty and very elegant. One of the women, whose dress I was admiring suggested that I take a very close look at the lace in her dress. Upon closer scrutiny, I burst into laughter. The design woven into the elegant sheer black lace was none other than a very familiar character—Mickey Mouse!

It was very much a thrill to be invited by my friend Nadia to her village and her sister's home. Nubian villages are private and it is rare to see anyone except residents and family there. It's extremely rare to see a tourist in a traditional Nubian village.

Unlike many typical Egyptian towns and villages, Nubian villages are very clean and homes are painted and well cared for. Homes are attractive and nicely decorated with ethnic designs, even though they are made from the same building materials as Egyptian homes.

It's traditional among Nubian women to wear henna for festive occasions. Henna powder is used for painting tattoo-like designs on body parts. The powder comes from the dried leaves of the henna plant—a shrub or small flowering tree. This has been used as a body decoration or hair color enhancer since antiquity.

As a gift to me, Nadia asked one of the village women, who is a henna artist to do some of her best work on me. First she tore a page out of a book and rolled it so that it made a cone with a very small spout on one end. This became her brush. Then the henna powder had to be finely sifted to remove all lumps, but there was nothing in the house with which to sift. So, a curtain was taken off the window and the loosely woven fabric was used to sift the lumps from the henna powder. When it was mixed with water, forming a paste, and placed into the paper cone, the artist was ready to go to work.

Once the designs were drawn on my hands, arms, and feet they dried almost instantly in the 100 degree desert heat. But in order to emphasize them and to make them last much longer, I needed to bake this henna into my skin. A small charcoal fire was made in a metal container which was set on the floor under a wooden chair. A blanket was draped over the entire set-up, creating a "smoker oven." So as each limb of my body was painted I placed that limb under the blanket or *into the oven* for about fifteen minutes.

All told, it took about six hours to complete the entire process. During this time village women were coming and going in and out of the house, admiring the work of the artist and satisfying their curiosity about what henna looks like on white skin. Most Nubians have very dark skin. Mine looked beautiful and because I treated my henna designs very gently, they lasted about two weeks.

A Nubian Experience

For three years running my Nubian friend Nadia has invited me to join the folks from her village in southern Egypt in their annual fund-raiser celebration. Of course, I am the only non-Nubian in the crowd and the cultural experience could never be equaled.

The villagers commission a rather old and beat-up car ferry for the day and they set sail from the little Nubian town of KomOmbo heading upriver to tourist-popular Aswan. This is not your ordinary sail; but one that includes a great group of Nubian musicians, 3 professional singers, BIG amplifiers and non-stop Nubian dancing all the way—for all six hours of the journey. Being a car ferry, but having no cars, it looks and sounds like a giant dance floor slowly moving up the river.

Nubian dancing and music are unlike typical Egyptian music and dancing. They have more of an African sound. It's really fun to watch and the men dance far more than the women, as at Egyptian parties.

The amplified music could be heard throughout all the villages along the way and people ran toward the river bank when they heard us coming. Once the ferry reached the people, the music became contagious and soon there was dancing all along the banks of the Nile also.

A number of years ago I took Hanem, Sayeed and Jamalat's daughter, to this event. It was twelve year old Hanem's first excursion outside her village. Unfortunately, drinks of any sort were not sold on this ferry and one got rather thirsty. So when young Hanem offered me a glass of steaming hot tea, I was overjoyed. I sure needed a quick pick-me-up and I drank it almost straight down, never questioning where the water for the tea came from—although I knew it could only come from one place.

I got my answer very shortly. Of course, it had to come from the river and there lying in the Nile, just a few feet directly upstream, was a decomposing dead camel. Many people believe that if a visitor to this land drinks from the Nile, it guarantees their return to Egypt. Well, it worked for me!

Pizza

We were visiting an elderly auntie and usually the conversation was rather limited because she didn't keep up with current events, and wasn't educated or knowledgeable. Somehow the word "pizza" was mentioned and Auntie, quite wrinkled and shriveled and swathed in black from head to toe, requested that we bring her a pizza next time we visit.

I was totally shocked at the request, so I said, "Oh Auntie, you *like* pizza?" But Auntie was one step ahead of me. "Oh no," she said. "I just want to see what one looks like."

Hani's Pride

Hani spoke just a little English. At age 37, he had a good job, a nice family, and was well respected in his community. He was very proud that he had a more prestigious position than his brothers. One day he asked me, "Madame Jonna, the United States is very very?" I knew this was a serious question and I felt it deserved a serious answer, so I waited for the sentence to be completed.

When I realized that the sentence *was* complete, my thoughts raced. Yes, the United States is very good and very bad, it is very hot and very cold, it is very rich and very poor, it is very strong and very weak, etc. So, my answer was as simple as his question: "Yes, the United States *is* very very," I said.

He burst into an ear-to-ear smile, filled with pride, and almost danced as he confirmed, "I know it! I know it! I know I right!"

Displays of Affection

Sometimes visitors to Upper Egypt are shocked and surprised to see men in displays of affection. It is very much against the culture for a man and a woman to publicly show affection, but it is readily acceptable for men or women to walk along the streets holding hands or with an arm around each other. This may be a father and son or it may be two best friends. When walking with an Egyptian lady friend, we always walk arm in arm or hand in hand. I love to see the young children walking to and from school, holding hands.

For men, a typical greeting is a kiss on each cheek rather than a handshake, as in the west. The same holds true for the women embracing each other. Typically an Egyptian man and woman do not shake hands and would never embrace in the way men and women embrace the same sex. A woman should always offer her hand first if a handshake is in order.

On some occasions I have offered my hand upon introduction, only to be refused a handshake by the man. Either he was one who did not believe in any kind of touching between male and female, or he was washed and ready for prayers and did not want to contaminate himself by touching me.

Airport Meeting in Cairo

Upon my return to Egypt from a visit to America in 1994, I was being met at the Cairo International Airport (CAI) by Mosleh, whom I did not know, but he is a friend of a friend. Before leaving America I had one telephone conversation with Mosleh and told him precisely how I would be dressed, including the color of my skirt and blouse and shoes. Though I had no idea how to identify him, I was sure he would be able to spot me immediately. After all, I don't look like an Egyptian and my very fair skin and western features advertise that I am a tourist. There would be no problems.

Being met at the airport by an Egyptian man is very common. Usually he will be a guide, or a representative of a hotel, or a driver. All these men carry a sign announcing who they represent, or identifying the arriving tourist for whom they are searching. They usually number thirty to forty and they line the corridor inside the airport and greet their parties before the tourist even goes through customs. They are dressed in western fashion and all speak another language in addition to Arabic. They are orderly, helpful, polite and very friendly.

Usually I would scurry as quickly as possible through this line-up of sign-carrying men, looking neither to the right nor to the left. On that morning I walked slowly, reading every sign. I wanted to be seen. No one beckoned to me. In fact, I was completely ignored. Not one of these men welcomed me to Egypt. Where was Mosleh? What had come over them? This was very unusual.

Finally I had no choice but to go into the terminal where Egyptians would be patiently waiting for their own loved ones. All the other tourists had already gone in the opposite direction, into the mad crush of taxi drivers, hotel representatives, water vendors, and who-knows-what-else, shouting out their "cheap price" or beckoning loudly for fares, while the dispatcher tried to keep some semblance of order.

Compared to other international airports, the CAI was very small and devoid of amenities. Though millions of tourists visited Egypt each year, there was no paging system in this airport in 1994. Today CAI is a series of new and very beautiful ultra-modern terminals—a feast for the senses and a pleasure to fly in and out of.

The best thing for me to do, I reasoned, was to put myself in a very conspicuous place so that Mosleh could easily see me. As the Egyptians sat or stood around the perimeter of the room, I placed myself in dead center, so I could be seen by everyone. I stood. I waited. I shifted from one foot to the other. I walked in circles. I looked at everyone. No one looked at me. It was as if I was invisible.

Based on experiences from the past, I knew that Mosleh was in that room, or soon would be in that room. I also knew that he would wait hours for me, if that's how long it took. But why wasn't he acknowledging me? It would be *my* responsibility to find *him.*

Which one of the one hundred or so men would be Mosleh? I recalled that he said he originally came from a small village in the south of Egypt—Upper Egypt. Generally speaking, Egyptians in the south have darker skin color than Egyptians in the north. This was how my search began. I approached men with darker skin and asked them if their name was Mosleh. Even though I asked in Arabic, my American accent should have been a real give-away. Every man answered a very polite, "No," without making eye contact with me.

Finally, I approached one short, dark skinned man who said, "Yes, I am Mosleh." When I told him that I was Jonna, he responded with an emphatic, "No! You are not Jonna. You cannot be Jonna. You are an Egyptian woman. I am here to meet an American."

I had forgotten to mention to Mosleh that I would have my hair covered in the Egyptian fashion and that my skirt would be ankle length—same as all Egyptian women. I was not dressed in American blue jeans as he expected. Wearing the *hijab* (head covering) and long skirt had changed everyone's attitude toward me. They thought I was an Egyptian woman. It took me some time to process all of this in my own mind.

A proper Egyptian man does not approach or speak to an Egyptian woman outside his family. It would be extremely unusual for an Egyptian woman to ask an unknown man for help. Had I not been wearing *hijab*—had my head covered—nearly every man along the corridor and in the waiting room would have been trying to assist me. Egyptian men want to be helpful to foreign women, sometimes to an annoying degree. They understand that our western culture does not prevent them from approaching and speaking to us.

The message was obvious. The advantages of covering *could* outweigh the disadvantages. I determined that the *hijab* would cover my hair during my time in Egypt anytime I was out in public. As I visited and accepted invitations from women friends I displayed modesty. I felt secure that my scarf saved both men and women from embarrassment because I looked no different from any other woman. I blended in. I showed respect—but most important, I respected myself.

Wearing the hijab also helped keep hustlers at bay. Having my head covered in the style of Egypt put forth the question: is she or isn't she? They could not tell for sure if I was Egyptian and the Egyptian men didn't want to risk hassling one of their own.

There were a few other fringe benefits, as well. When I wore the hijab, men of every age who knew that I was a western woman, lavished compliments upon me—always telling me how beautiful I am. Covering my hair was economically beneficial too—the merchants very often offered me a nice discount "because you cover," they explained. One of the greatest personal benefits, however: I never had to worry about having a bad hair day. I just covered it up!

Goha

G oha is a likeable folk literature character throughout the
Middle East. He's somewhat of a simpleton or a fool and
everyone has a laugh at Goha's expense. There are many Goha stories in
Egypt, and here is one of my favorites.

Goha sat under the hazelnut tree trying to figure out one of life's
mysteries: why did God create such a very large tree to grow the very
small hazelnut and why did God create such a very small vine to grow
the very large watermelon? Goha overtaxed his brain thinking about
this mystery and he fell asleep sitting under the tree. He awakened with
a start when a little hazelnut fell on his head. "Now I understand the
wisdom of God. If this big tree gave forth watermelons, that would have
been the end of me," declared Goha.

Gas Jeans

Egyptians wearing western style clothing seem to love having English printing on their clothing. Most often their clothing is a very cheap knock-off of some major brand and probably not one Egyptian knows what it really says. I amuse myself by reading these, as most are mistakes. One that I had a private chuckle over was a knock-off for Guess Jeans, but in big bold letters, across the rear, it said "Gas Jeans." I wonder if the cocky young man in the jeans had any idea what this might imply.

One at a Time

For a person who is accustomed to buying in bulk—or at least, the large economy size, I find buying in Egypt quite comical at times. If I want to bake a cake and I need 2 cups flour and 2 teaspoons baking powder and 2 eggs, that is exactly what I buy. Everybody shops like that. So by the time I get home with these items, my cake is just about ready for the oven.

Until the past year I had to visit a different kiosk to buy each of those items. New to Luxor is the supermarket! Though nothing on the scale of what most of us in the west are accustomed to, it still is a supermarket and business is very good! It's about half the size of my entire flat. People of Luxor love it. People on the west bank of the river are just a little less enthused about it. They prefer spending less money and not having to concern themselves with where to store the item.

But now I am required to buy in packages and I have to do all the measuring myself when I bake. Then I have to put away all the packages and it has cost me a lot more than it did before.

Walking to the ferry, my shoe strap rubbed my foot in a most uncomfortable way, so I stopped at the pharmacy and purchased one band aid. Yes, a single band aid. I guess I'll do the same next time it hurts. Why buy an entire package if I only need one?

Bedrooms

Here in Egypt, bedrooms are not the sacred territory that they often are in the west. It isn't unusual to entertain guests in the bedroom, using the bed as a place for sitting. Others sit on the bedroom floor. I've been in homes where this room is used as the room for eating, especially if guests are present. A bedroom might have as many beds as can possibly be squeezed into the space and there is nothing personal about this room. It's merely a place to close one's eyes and get a night's rest.

Many homes don't have a separate bedroom, so the entire family sleeps in the main entry room, called the *reception.* The sturdy wooden benches that serve as couches for seating during the day become beds for sleeping at night. If there are not enough benches to accommodate everyone, then some family members sleep on the floor which is a very common and acceptable practice. Many homes in the villages do not even own a mattress. Villagers might go through life never experiencing the comfort of a mattress.

There are many customs here that take a bit of getting used to. But there is one custom I just find totally amusing. When Omran and I entertain family or close friends, following the afternoon meal our guests crawl onto one of our beds and take a long nap. The beds in our home are all queen size, so that will accommodate at least three persons on each bed. No announcements made; no permission requested, no questions asked.

I questioned my husband about this and he said this is a sign of respect and honor—if you don't like someone, you certainly don't want to sleep in their bed. Maybe this explains why friends are always inviting me to sleep at their home—even when my own home is directly across the street.

Rain, Rain, Go Away

Taking a lot for granted, I said to a Cairo friend, "I bet you love it when rain comes to your city and cools it down and washes everything clean." To my astonishment, he replied "Absolutely not! It's horrible! The water turns the dust on the trees to mud, dripping all over us when we walk under or near the trees, ruining our clothing. It creates a slick surface on the sidewalks and the streets, causing people to slip and fall and cars to slide about, creating accidents." He went on with his dislikes, but I got the message in the first couple of sentences.

Cairo Visit

In 1922 when archaeologist Howard Carter peered for the first time into the newly discovered tomb of Pharaoh Tutankhamen, he was questioned by a very anxious Lord Carnarvan. Naturally, Carnarvan, in his business suit and tie, was standing by with the obvious question. "What do you see?" Answered Carter, "I see wonderful things." This may be the understatement of the century.

I thought of this scenario as I experienced Cairo this week. It's difficult to know where or how to begin talking about the magnitude of the surroundings, the numbers of people, the overwhelming busyness of this city of twenty million people—the largest city on the African continent, also the largest city in the Middle East. Still, I felt safe, comfortable and totally at ease.

It is easy to understand why, for centuries, Cairo has been called "the city of a thousand *minarets*," but less easy for me to understand why it is also known as "the mother of all cities."

This busy place is not new to me; I am more comfortable here than in any other major world city—although it still swallows me. It is a city I love to hate. I know my way around. I enjoy Cairo. The people are friendly and helpful. At the same time, after a few days I am ready to scream, "Get me out of here!" It has recently been given the title of one of the few cities in the world that never sleeps.

In my American hometown I often lecture about Egypt, and I describe the capital city something like this: a great big polluted, smelly, dirty, overcrowded, noisy, traffic-snarled, wonderful, exciting, generous, mysterious, magical, friendly city. We made the trip to *Masr* (the Arabic word for Cairo) to visit Omran's recently married sister and so that I could meet her husband. They live in a suburb, about an hour away via the metro and a short taxi ride.

Omran's mother wanted so badly to go with us but Omran didn't want this responsibility. He got his first opportunity to see what married life is *really* like: I overruled him. So *Om Gozi* traveled with us.

Omran was responsible for our baggage and I was responsible for *Om Gozi*, sitting with her, squeezing her hand through metro stops, railway stations and crossing busy streets. She loved all this special attention. The big city was overwhelming to her; as it was to all of us. I was fearful that if I let go of her hand, for even an instant, I'd lose her forever in the sea of slow moving black-clad women. They all looked the same—the only thing making them identifiable was the small amount of flesh that showed if one was viewing them straight on, directly from the front. Definitely they could not be identified by their apparel. I think Omran had the easiest job!

My husband is a very typical Upper Egyptian in that he knows nothing about the city and has no idea what attractions are there. He had never visited the pyramids or a museum, and would never choose to do so. Since I'm a history enthusiast and have never seen a museum I didn't like, I introduced him to a whole new experience. Once we got Om Gozi settled into the home of her daughter in the suburbs, I was free to enjoy entertaining Omran with the delights of his own capital city.

I knew that the wonderful museum of Egyptian antiquities, to which I am so devoted, would be of no real interest to him, and I'd best find a point of interest he could easily relate to and identify with. So after a visit to the Egyptian Military Museum, I (the non-Muslim) took him (the Muslim) to visit Cairo's largest and most famous mosque—the

Masjid of Mohammed Ali—a place of special beauty and tranquility and my favorite. I wish his mother had been with us as neither of them had been in any place of worship except their tiny village mosque, built of mud bricks and completely unadorned.

After choosing places of interest for Omran, I decided it was time to visit an area of Cairo where I don't often have the courage to go: Al Muskie. This is a place where Egyptians shop, where the best prices can be found and it is so jam packed with people that one must push one's way through the crowds. The people are so thickly packed that getting an automobile down one of Al Muskie's streets is such an unrealistic thought that cars don't even try and the people use the streets for their walkways.

I was standing at an intersection when someone yelled "police." Instantly, out of the crowd in the street a half dozen six feet long tables, covered with merchandise, raised up high into the air and went moving very fast down the street, the men carrying the tables yelling at shoppers to move aside. These were some of the unlicensed merchants who regularly do business there. They turned, went down an alley, circled around and came right back and sat their tables down where they began—the police had now moved on from this area.

The young Egyptian merchant that I had been negotiating with also disappeared when the police arrived, leaving me standing on the corner holding a large brown paper sack stuffed full of beautiful silk scarves. He would never find me in that crowd and I wondered what I would do with his merchandise. Suddenly, there he was right in front of me, wearing the same smile he had on when he disappeared, and we continued our conversation as if nothing had disrupted it. I negotiated a price good enough for me to buy six new silk scarves from a merchant whose outlet was a brown paper bag.

We did not spend most of our time in tourist Cairo, but were invited to the homes of some of Omran's recent army buddies where I saw a lot of the city that I had not experienced previously—the peoples' Cairo. It was fun meeting new Cairenes and seeing Omran and his pals rekindle their relationships.

The trip from Luxor to Cairo is about twelve hours by express train. Even though we had seats in the first class car, we had to sit up all night. There is an overnight sleeper train, but it is too expensive for most Egyptians to use. Mostly it is for tourists. Who wouldn't enjoy lying in bed and watching the Egyptian Nile countryside slide by in the moonlight?

Cairo Traffic

Imagine for a moment that you are driving to or from work and there are no lines on the pavement showing traffic lanes, no double yellows, no turn lanes and no signage. Now imagine there are no red and green traffic lights or stop signs. Cars are entering from side streets often without benefit of stopping or waiting their turn, or slowing down. Pedestrians, including young children, are running in front of you, trying to cross the street. Imagine that in the mass of autos there are also bicycles, motorcycles, horse drawn carriages, donkey carts or maybe even a herd of camels on the way to market. It's dark now and not one car has its lights on, or intends to turn them on. Street vendors dash between autos in the multilane traffic, quickly stuffing their wares through the open windows trying to make a quick sale. Now imagine an additional three million vehicles in the streets. This is Cairo, my friends, and none of this is a product of the imagination. It is very real.

Traffic on the Cairo streets is horrendously legendary. There simply are too many automobiles for the size of the streets. There's no place to park, so it is common for drivers to park on the sidewalks, or more likely, they just stop where they are and consider themselves parked. The number of traffic lights in this city of twenty million people could be counted on one hand. No matter because drivers ignore all signs and lights. Traffic usually moves along at a respectable speed. A driver's objective is to keep enough distance between his auto and the one in front of him so that he can stop in a fraction of a second, but this distance must never be enough for another vehicle to cut in and fill the space. When driving on an exit ramp or a one-way street, never assume that all traffic will be going the same direction. I once witnessed a car backing up the down-sloping exit ramp. If a driver wishes to make a right turn he does not get into the so-called right lane, as it is moving too slowly. Rather he gets into the next lane, but still turns right, crossing in front of all traffic. There are no rules so no tickets or citations are issued.

Taxi drivers, with all their experience, are quite comfortable behind the wheel. If the driver is friendly and helpful to me, chances are that I'll tip him well. In his efforts to befriend me, he turns so he can look me in the eye in the back seat, as he leads our chatter and laughter. He spends more time looking backward than looking forward. More than once I've yelled and he applied the brake just in the nick of time.

It is often difficult for drivers to concentrate on the traffic because of the many distractions on the streets. I was in the back seat of a taxi, near the slaughterhouse district, when suddenly both the driver and I let out a yell that said, "No, it can't be!" There in the traffic next to us, and a few yards ahead, was a naked cow riding a bicycle. It had been stripped of its hide, but how does a cow ride a bicycle?

As we got close enough for a better look, we saw that a young man was actually pedaling the cycle and he was apparently transporting this whole, freshly butchered beef to his place of business, perhaps a restaurant or a retail store. How else would he get such a heavy load to its destination except to drape it over himself or to crawl inside and wear it?

If there are no required stops for the traffic and no pedestrian crosswalks, then how do the people manage to cross the multilane streets? My first few times crossing the street were so terrifying I worked my way into a small group of Egyptian citizens, getting as close to one of them as I possibly could without getting arrested. Instead of looking at the traffic, I watched my fellow pedestrians and moved exactly when they moved and stopped exactly when they stopped. I still depend on that method to get me safely across the busy streets, but I hope I'm not quite so obvious about it.

Basically, one just sizes up the traffic flow and then at the chosen moment, steps out into the traffic and begins walking. Somehow the cars and those on foot seem to time it just right and everyone manages to cross unscathed, but just barely. I know a man whose toes were run over as he tried to cross the street. I've decided that if one chooses his pace, and does not slow down or rush, drivers will do the same. Now, I am brave enough to step out in front of an automobile, but not yet brave enough to challenge a bus.

I really enjoy bringing groups of tourists to Egypt to visit the antiquities. I am constantly asked by westerners, "Is it safe to travel in Egypt? Aren't you scared to take people to Egypt? Don't you fear for your life?" My answer is always, "Yes. I am terrified when in Egypt; my greatest fear is trying to move a group of tourists across the Cairo streets." As often as possible, I find a policeman who will go out into the street and stop the traffic so that my group can cross. Of course, it costs us a hefty tip, but it is well worth it and I am happy to pay up!

An Egyptian friend told me that "a green signal means go and red means go like hell!" Another driver told me traffic signals are merely a suggestion. Yet a third said that a yellow light means to slow down a little and think about it. There's a saying in Egypt that you can drive a car without brakes, but you cannot drive a car without a horn. The language of the horn is used not just to say *"get out of the way,"* but to give important information to the other drivers.

One newspaper article I read said "The traffic here is so bad those of a faint disposition will not survive the daily commute." Sadly, many don't. Annually about one thousand Cairenes are killed and four thousand more are injured on city streets. It is near impossible for an emergency vehicle to get through the traffic, so other motorists take care of the situation in whatever way they deem best for the moment. Outside of Cairo the situation isn't much better, although there's less traffic. I've never seen a highway patrol or an emergency vehicle on an Egyptian road.

Everyone agrees that something needs to be done about the traffic, but that seems like a minor issue now with all the other problems Egypt is facing. So this country remains the world's leader in traffic accidents with forty times more than the US. My own belief is that if all these drivers stopped regularly for traffic lights and signs, as in the west, that Cairo would be a colossal traffic jam. What keeps the traffic flowing is every drivers' obsession to be in front of the car ahead of him.

At the Luxor Hospital

Luxor was quiet and uneventful during the 2011 political uprising in Cairo and it was equally quiet during the resignation of President Mubarak and the victory celebrations. The people of Upper Egypt feel as if they are far removed from all that happens politically, and no matter what they think or say their lives will not be changed. A change in Cairo will not put bread in their mud-brick ovens tomorrow. So, why get excited or worked up?

We celebrated by going out to a new coffee house, along with Hammam and Mahmood, cousins to each other and same-age nephews of Omran, all from his village and all living just a few doors apart. It's difficult to find someone in their village that is not related to Omran; his grandfather sired twenty-two sons, all with the same wife.

There was no celebrating the next evening. Omran spent that time at the Luxor International Hospital, a rather large operation, government owned of course, sitting and praying with the family. Mahmood wrecked his motorcycle that day and had such serious leg breaks that he had to be transported to the hospital in Luxor. *Ilhamdu lil Allah,* this could actually be done by ambulance. That would not have been possible a few years ago.

In late 1997 the first Nile crossing bridge opened about ten miles south of Luxor and that allowed joining the east bank and the west bank of Luxor via motor traffic. Before that time, there was a people's ferry and a car ferry, so it was not impossible to cross the Nile in a motor vehicle—perhaps just not quite as convenient. The car ferry appeared to be a big floating parking lot—just a large flat surface with a simple railing all the way around. No more than that. The drivers and perhaps a few other individuals accompanied the automobiles.

But I saw the car ferry once with a most unusual cargo. There were no cars on it because it was crammed full with a large herd of camels. Now camels are accustomed to solid earth under foot and sand between the toes of their hooves, so it was obviously a very bewildering experience for them. Camels have a habit of stretching their neck and looking around in a way that no other animal does. They appeared bewildered. I'm sure they couldn't figure out why they were moving while their feet stood still. It was very amusing to watch and it was probably the last time a large herd of camels crossed the Nile at Luxor riding on a car ferry. This particular floating device is now just a memory.

The people's ferry still is the most practical, least expensive, quickest, safest, most frequent means of transportation. The east and west docks are a straight shot across the River Nile, where the water is about a half mile wide. The people's ferry runs continuously, almost twenty-four hours, and has a capacity of about one hundred to one hundred-fifty passengers. A ferry usually departs the dock as the next full one arrives. Unless the time is the middle of the night, the ferry is always full.

Today, when I leave Luxor, go ten miles south, drive the mile across the bridge, then travel ten miles north again, I wonder about the practicality of using the bridge. I've driven twenty-one miles to get directly across the Nile. But when it is possible to get nephew Mahmood to the hospital in a reasonably quick time, I am most grateful.

Later, Omran and I together visited his nephew in the hospital in Luxor. I'm still shocked and in disbelief that we were required to pay an entrance fee to visit someone in the hospital. I cannot accept that as anywhere near the norm, but perhaps it's the going thing and I am not up with the times. The entrance fee to visit a loved one is two Egyptian pounds during regular visiting hours. But if one can't make it during that time, then ten Egyptian pounds will open the doors upon request. Remember, this is Egypt where most business transactions involve money *under the table*. It appears this hospital is getting rich from these entrance fees and the man selling the entrance tickets may be getting richer.

It is common for all family, no matter how distant, to visit any hospitalized loved one so all rooms are usually full of visiting women with children and the halls are filled with the waiting male family members—at times, so many that it is difficult to navigate the corridors. The men do visit the patient before they take up their positions in the halls; they just need less time than the women. But it's a good time to visit with family and to catch up on the family news and gossip.

There are four beds in Mahmood's room, each holding a man recovering from a motorcycle accident and each nursing quite severe broken bones. Consider that each man's family and friends are also in the room, but most of the men are occupying the hallway. Also, consider that it's a rather small room but the adjoining balcony catches the overflow, which includes all of the cigarette smokers, and that's most of the men. Yet, the patients are lying in their hospital beds, smoking up a storm!

I wore my usual clothing consisting of a colorful floor length full skirt with a coordinating long sleeve top. My hair was covered in a silk scarf that I had tied in one of the fancy regional styles. I was the only female I saw inside or outside the hospital who was not swathed in a black *abaya* and black *hijab*, cascading to the ground. In the moonlight these women create an eerie sight, slowly moving about the hospital grounds like black ghosts on a black background, and then disappearing into the black shadows. One Egyptian man referred to them as "moving tents."

Rules of the Road: Motorcycles

Much of the body movement when some Egyptian men dance is from the waist up, moving the chest, shoulders, arms and hands. So it is not unusual to see a motorcyclist racing along at high speed, earphones firmly in place, while "dancing" from the waist up. His hands are well above his head, moving to the rhythm of the music, with no one driving the motorcycle.

Common usage of motorcycles and motorbikes is relatively new to Egypt. A fairly inexpensive model is being imported now from China and is available to more and more Egyptians, who are adept at making their own traffic rules. Accidents are frequent. No one uses a protective helmet; there are many underage drivers and none are properly trained. High speed appears to be necessary, even through the narrow dirt lanes of the village where toddlers are playing about and old men and women are walking or sitting on door steps.

Three adults on a motorcycle is a very common sight, but my heart jumps into my throat when I see a family of six on a motorcycle. The women ride sidesaddle behind the male driver and I've seen a mother nursing an infant while riding like this. One bike was so laden with passengers that a small child had to stand on an adult lap, as there was no space for the little guy to sit.

Flashing Lights

Try as I might, even after twenty-some years of being in Egypt, I still cannot get comfortable with automobiles and motorcycles being driven at night without the lights turned on. No matter if the vehicle is in the City of Cairo or a tiny village, on a major highway or a small town back street. No matter if there's a full moon and stars; or a sliver of a moon and no stars. I still find it very scary when I'm in a car with no lights and suddenly encounter a motorcycle with no lights. Donkeys wandering on the road or a donkey and rider are more commonplace even than motorcycles. When women, clad in layers of black from the top of the head to the toes, walk on the road after dark, they are impossible to see.

In defense of the drivers, they seem to be quite alert when in these dark situations and it is common practice to give the headlights a very quick flash if they are aware of oncoming traffic. It's just to say, "Hey, I'm over here." The purpose of driving without lights is also a very practical one. One's vehicle lights could temporarily blind the oncoming driver and cause an accident. After they "flash" the oncoming vehicle, they politely turn off the lights again. Very scary.

If drivers psychologically miss anything by not using headlights on the car, they make up for it with the horn. In fact, the horn is in such constant use that it is often attached to the steering wheel at the two o'clock position, so the driver's hand is always in contact with it.

There is a saying amongst Egyptians: You can drive a car without brakes, but you cannot drive a car without a horn. That may sound funny, but it is *no* joke!

There is a language of the horns and if one listens carefully and is observant enough, it is relatively easy to figure out this language. Two short beeps say "Hey, I'm over here. Be careful." One long loud blast of the horn says exactly what you would expect: "Get out of the way, I'm coming through." If the car behind wants to pass, the driver will signal that it is not safe by putting his hand out the window, fingers together and pointed upward. If it is safe to pass, that hand signal will motion to come on. All that horn blowing on Egypt's terribly overcrowded streets and by-ways is quite annoying.

When driving outside the major cities, it is never necessary to wait until there is no oncoming traffic before passing the vehicle in front. When a car pulls into the oncoming lane in preparation for passing, all approaching vehicles simply move over, often going onto the shoulder. The passing car goes straight down the center of the two lane highway. Drivers are consistently polite and cooperative with these road manners.

The Hot Air Balloons are Back

O mran yelled excitedly from the terrace of our rented house on the edge of the *sahara,* "The balloons are back! The balloons are back!" Indeed, the balloons *were* back and what a pretty sight it was—even at five-thirty in the morning. We had no idea the colorful hot air balloons for the tourists would return on this day, and to look across the desert, just beyond our garden, and see these six colorful giant balls floating through the air lifted our hearts. We savored this sight as we drank our morning tea, sitting in our garden and watching the daily sunrise to the east, as last night's moon slipped out of sight on the other side.

The six hot air balloons had not flown all summer. It was very tranquil to watch them silently moving, yet motionless at the same time. The desert appears so colorless, even against the rising sun, that these giants added an exciting splash of brightness.

Over the years I had often enjoyed a close-up view of the special places in these desert mountains while hiking or exploring from the back of a donkey. But when I took my first balloon ride, I was not prepared for the manner in which the sights affected me. Looking up at them from our garden terrace would not compare with watching the ground recede as my balloon moved higher and higher. At one point I had the thought: *This is God's viewpoint. I'm trespassing into God's territory.*

When I'm hiking down there with my feet firmly on the ground, the mountain does not appear as frightening as it does when I take in its massive entirety from the air. Some of the cliffs have a drop of more than one hundred feet. Sometimes I wonder, how could I have taken my donkey *there*? Or perhaps it should be the other way around: how could my donkey have taken me there?

My emotions erupt when I experience exquisite beauty I can't describe, such as looking at a masterpiece of art work, seeing a perfect rose, or listening to Andrea Bocelli singing Ave Maria. The grandeur of this desert is certainly one of God's masterpieces.

Mohamed Comes to Call

Omran's four and a half year old nephew lives in the family home with his mother and two unmarried aunts and his grandma. Early one morning I heard young Mohamed calling "Baba" (his name for Omran, the only Papa he knows) from our back terrace so I figured the entire family was coming for an unscheduled visit. We waited but no one showed up and upon questioning, we discovered that Mohamed had come through two villages, crossed a busy highway and walked across the desert all alone and, of course, had not informed anyone he was coming here.

Besides getting lost, the greatest dangers for him were possibly the packs of large wild dogs and jackals that roam the desert and attack anything that moves, as well as the scorpions and snakes. Because all the village people are part of Omran's family, everyone got involved, if only to spread the word and talk about the incident. Remember, there's not a lot of news here, so every little thing is treated as a big deal.

Little Mohamed goes twice a week to a pre-school/kindergarten. The teacher asked all the kids to stand and tell who their father is and what their father does for his occupation. This must be very difficult for this little guy, as he has almost no contact with his biological father and insists that Uncle Omran is his father. So to this question Mohamed answered, "My father is Omran and he married a tourist." Mohamed is very proud of this accomplishment.

I've been teaching Mohamed English, but he doesn't know this. I want it to come naturally to him. His mother phoned the other day, very excited, because she asked Mohamed a question and he responded in English. She doesn't speak English, so she handed the phone to him and Mohamed told me his response. He can find and say all the letters on the computer keyboard to spell his name in English, but as yet he doesn't get them all in the right order.

Little Mohamed often escorts me when I'm traveling around the west bank. Though I've been riding in these vans and pick-up trucks for more years than Mohamed has to his credit, it is comforting to have him so dutifully and responsibly looking after me. His attention mimics what he has seen and heard from the older men, especially his Uncle Omran. He tells me where to sit when entering a van and then arranges the seat for me, if necessary. He helps me up and down the steps if he feels I might need it. When we are about to cross the street, little Mohamed stretches his arm in front of me to force me to stop while he looks both ways for traffic. Mohamed's outstretched arm reaches just below my knees, but I know what that signal means. If he thinks I need my hand held, he does that too.

Holiday Depression

The Islamic calendar is a lunar calendar, so holidays do not always fall on the same yearly date as many of our holidays in the west tend to do. This year, however, a couple of very important celebrations fell on or near the same date as a couple of important American holidays: Thanksgiving and Christmas. As families here looked forward to this time of family gathering and the excitement of the approaching holiday grew, I became depressed, as I missed my family and friends in the west more and more.

There is no sign of Christmas here in Upper Egypt, as this population is over ninety percent Sunni Muslim. The Christians who do live here celebrate this important day on January 7. I imagine there is some indication of the holiday in the five-star hotels, but I don't go around those places. I heard some Christmas carols on CNN and burst into tears. There are no lights, no conifer trees, not even a street corner Santa ringing his bell and holding out his bucket. Definitely, there is no wintry weather that I have come to associate with Christmas.

As I began to plan my schedule for Christmas Eve and Christmas Day, I included time for spiritual reflection as I decided that would be the emphasis for my thoughts. It would give me a focus point and help me overcome my moodiness. However, when we received an invitation for a party, I decided a little African music and some dancing might do more to lift my spirits. I could do both.

The party was at the roof top restaurant and bar of a popular west bank hotel overlooking the Nile and right into the well-lighted Luxor Temple on the opposite bank. It was very well attended and I was happy to see a number of my Egyptian friends there. The buffet was plentiful and tasty, alcohol was available, but the music and dancing are the highlights of any party in Egypt.

Five different groups provided the evenings music—each a different style. My favorites will always be the music of the Sayeede or Upper Egyptian and the music of Nubia—very African. Three different belly dancers entertained at different times and a Whirling Dervish balanced out the evening. EVERYBODY danced the night away!

I have never felt like I'm a sensation on the dance floor, but once the drumming begins, my body will not sit still and it's common to dance every dance. The instruments for one Nubian music group consisted of only three different drums—nothing else. Omran is a marvelous dancer and I enjoy being his partner.

At the Farm House

The City of Luxor sits on the East Bank of the Nile. Most farmers and peasants—the *fellahin*—live on the West Bank. I went with a friend on the west side to visit her relatives on a remote farm. Since spending many happy childhood years on my own family's farm, I always enjoyed this atmosphere and felt very comfortable there. This farm was a little different than the farm where I grew up.

The water buffalo, chickens, ducks, pigeons, turkeys, rabbits and goats all lived in the family house. They had their own room but they used the family front door, just like everyone else. During my recent visit, as I sat there, I just had to stop and look around, get up and walk outside, shake my head to try and clear it, then go back inside—all to make sure that what I was seeing and hearing was really happening.

All twelve family members, plus my friend and I, and a neighbor and another relative were there in the same small room. There was much talking and laughing and drinking tea and the six children ran about playing and making happy noises.

All the while the goats wandered in and out through the front door, baaing as they went through the house; the rabbits scampered from under one seating bench to another, trying not to get stepped on; the turkey gobbled loudly and looked confused; the hen announced that she had laid an egg—all the while avoiding the two family men who were prostrate on the floor, in the center of the room, saying their afternoon prayers.

I finally became comfortable with the entire situation until I looked up to see the young white pigeon, in a state of panic and fear, his eyes red with fright, riding the ceiling fan around and around, flapping his wings for balance—unable to get off. To everyone else in the room there was nothing even slightly unusual about the entire scene.

Upper Egypt: Mismar

In the early afternoon we joined the crowd walking to the village home of Omran's cousin, Ali Ibrihim, where a large luncheon was being served. Cousin Ali had much to celebrate this day and there would be partying into the night. The village women had been busy cooking all this day and part of the previous day. This luncheon was by invitation, but *no one* is ever turned away from the Egyptian table. As is customary outside of one's own home, the men eat in one room and the women eat together in another room.

Following Egyptian custom, there are no tables, no knives, forks or spoons, no chairs for seating, no plates or glasses, no napkins or decorative centerpiece. But there is an abundance of wonderfully delicious Egyptian traditional food and fresh bread to go with it. Everyone sits on the earthen floor of the mud brick home, circling a very polished large round aluminum tray on which the bowls of food have been placed. There may be four or five trays with six to eight persons at each tray. Each person takes a large chunk of bread, breaks it into small pieces, which he then uses to dip into the food before him, a bite at a time, everyone eating from the same bowl at the same time. The bread is used as the fork or spoon is used in the west—it transports the food from the serving dish to the mouth. Plates are not necessary.

Initially, to the western mind, this may not sound too sanitary, but I assure the reader that it is. The bite-size piece of bread is held with the first three fingers of the right hand, dipped into the food—with fingers never touching the food. The bread is then placed into the mouth—fingers never touching the lips. All the food is prepared in a way that makes it compatible with this dipping process. Nothing needs to be cut or spread or combined.

As soon as a diner has eaten his fill, he says "*Il hamdu lilAllah*"—thanks to God—and leaves the eating area. There is no long after-dinner conversation with coffee and dessert, as often occurs in the west. Another diner may sit down in the now vacant place and repeat the process all over again. There are no plates or utensils to clear away. Tea is usually served after a meal, but it is served away from the food.

I like eating in this manner. There is something warming and welcoming about sharing the same dishes at a common table. There is no passing of food, but there *is* a lot of reaching. From a woman's point of view, clean-up is easy.

Cousin Ali was giving this party to show his gratitude and thanksgiving for God's answered prayers. For the first few years of Ali's married life, he and his wife did not conceive a child. So Ali did what many have done—or might do. He made a promise to God: if he were granted children, he would do something special to honor the beloved local holy man, *Sheikh* Omran—who was also Ali's great grandfather and the great grandfather of my husband Omran. There are many ways to honor a beloved person, and Ali promised to name his first son after this well-loved deceased *sheikh*. He also promised God that, when he could afford it, he would have a grand *mismar* to publicly share his thanksgiving with all the people. God answered Ali's prayers and now he and his three sons—God's gifts—were leading this celebration of thanksgiving.

A *sheikh* is a very wise and learned man. He may be the village *sheikh*, and using his wisdom to more or less make sure things go smoothly—somewhat like a village mayor. Villagers come to the *sheikh* for advice and to settle disagreements. Another kind of *sheikh* is associated with the mosque and he usually has a university degree dealing with some phase of Islam. As long as he is diligent about seeking out knowledge from the Quran and continuing his studies, he can be called a *sheikh.* In the Arabic language the very word means *elder* and rarely does a man use this title before the age of forty or fifty.

As soon as everyone had finished eating the abundant lunch, six vans and an open pick-up truck appeared and at least seventeen adults plus little children crammed into each fourteen passenger van. That is, everyone except the five local musicians and the singer, who sat on plastic outdoor style chairs, in the back of the open pick-up truck, along with two male dancers. The turbaned musicians played, the singer performed and the *galabaya*-clad dancers danced as our little parade sped along the country lanes, beside the canals, through the date palm groves and bright green sugar cane fields until coming to a very old cemetery surrounding the dilapidated mausoleum of *Sheikh* Omran.

All the while, the six vans followed at top speed, with their very crowded passengers clapping and singing to the music and the drivers constantly blowing the horns. This is one of the ways Egyptians show that they are celebrating a happy occasion. The more noise, the better the celebration! It also serves as an invitation to come and join the fun. Egyptians are very welcoming.

I often marvel at the frequency and ease with which the rural Egyptians have fun. These are very hard working poor people, many of them *fellahin* (peasants), so money isn't a criterion for having fun. All that's needed is some music, or something to drum on, and the party begins.

The Tombs of the Nobles in Old Gurna Village, on the west bank, have very descriptive paintings depicting how the noble people partied and celebrated three thousand five-hundred years ago. There's even a scene showing an attractive young female partygoer throwing up, presumably after drinking too much beer, and the servant is there with a vessel to catch it, so as not to soil her beautiful dress. This indicates to me that this was a common happening, as beer was made in ancient Egyptian homes and drunk by all, even the children. It may have had somewhat different properties than our twenty-first century beer. When I'm partying on the west bank, surrounded by ancient monuments and temples and carved pictures of pharaonic era men and women, I often feel transported back a few thousand years, as if I've done this before.

But wait! *This* party was just beginning. At the mausoleum many of the women went inside to pray or pay their respect to the beloved holy man, *Sheikh* Omran. Outside, the musicians were giving it their all as the stick dancing had begun. Stick dancing is a ballet-like, slow motion, graceful, elegant dance, done with a partner and is favored by the older generation. It mimics ancient hand-to-hand combat between two warriors and is always danced to a special type of live music. The stick replaces the hand-held weapon of ancient times; therefore it is only performed by the men. The dance is actually a contest.

This is one dance in which youth *does not* have the advantage. This is a serious dance requiring much skill and fancy footwork, which can only be gained through years of practice and repetition. Stick dancing always draws a large crowd of admirers, as every village has its own favorites. Always there is a younger man in the crowd who challenges one of the older men. I've not yet seen a younger man beat his older competitor.

Stick dancing is always part of the *mismar*. After an hour or so of dancing at the mausoleum, the party-goers reversed their order and with the same music, clapping and singing, everyone returned to the home of Cousin Ali, where wooden benches lining the dirt lane in front of his house closed the street to traffic, and a hastily built bandstand awaited the musicians. For the next five hours the party and the dancing continued. The crowd grew while Ali's family continued to serve beverages and food to their honored guests.

Omran and I left the party in the wee hours of morning, completely "partied out." Without question, I felt that God had been well thanked and that *Sheikh* Omran had again been honored and I was happy to have been a part of all twelve hours of it.

Sufi Dancing or
Whirling Dervishes

In recent years a colorful religious ritual has been turned into
an act of entertainment. The Dervishes are Sufis who follow a
spiritual off-shoot of Islam, known for its mysticism, and who believe
that their trance-inducing whirling dancing leads to oneness with *Allah*.
Originally the garments worn by these Dervishes were made from
wool—the Arabic word is *suf.* They became known as Sufis.

Their dancing was never intended as entertainment, but it has
become a tourist attraction. I have never witnessed a private religious Sufi
ceremony, so I don't know if the same type of music is used. When this
event is for religious purposes, the colorful and entertaining skirts are not
worn, and the garments worn are pure white and not elaborate. This is a
sacred ritual and focuses on the relationship between body and soul, man
and God, lover and beloved, with submission to God. It should never
be hurried or rushed and the dancer might twirl round and round in a
counter clockwise direction for a very long time: hours, in fact.

As the Dervish whirls, his right arm is extended and raised, palm
pointing up toward the heavens while his left arm is lowered and
extended, with palm facing downward toward the earth. He is now
grounded or connected to both locations.

During a performance of a Whirling Dervish, I watched him whirl for forty-five continuous minutes, in a trance or trance-like state, never missing a step and never wavering. When he stopped dancing he walked away with a perfectly steady gait.

When the dance is performed as entertainment, the dancer wears two or more very colorful full length circular skirts, and while whirling perfectly, he manages to unfasten and remove the skirts from his waist and raise and twirl them high above his head in an entertaining manner, never losing his connection with God. The skirts puff full of air so that it often looks like a flying saucer hovering above the dancer's body.

Noise

E gypt is a very noisy place! There is no polite way to convey that message. The tranquil appearance of water buffalo pulling single blade plows through the fields, individuals quietly working the soil, black clad women walking slowly along the dirt road, oxen leisurely grazing, a fisherman sitting in his small boat on the Nile, rod limply held; and the peaceful look of the mud brick village are all deceiving. It is possible to know which day of the week we are experiencing from the variety of noise around us. I like best the happy sounds of Friday.

For most, every day begins between four and four-thirty with the first call to prayer. This is even before the rooster crows! In the Muslim world it is the custom to pray each day at five appointed times.

To help all people say their prayers at the proper intervals, a notice is blasted out from the top of each mosque's *minaret*. A *minaret* is the round cylinder-like, very tall, beautiful piece of architecture that stands far higher than the roof of the mosque. Some mosques have more than one *minaret*. Just a few years ago the *muezzin* (prayer leader) still climbed the circling stairs going high up into this minaret and called down to the people of the village or neighborhood, telling them it was now time to stop what they were doing and to devote this time to God—right where they were.

The *muezzin* still leads the prayers for every Egyptian within hearing range, though nowadays he is aided by loud speakers. If going to the mosque to pray is not practical, then one prays exactly where one is at the moment. So it is common to see men in the prayer positions, facing the holy city of Makka, in Saudi Arabia, in the most unusual public places: on city sidewalks, in fishing boats on the Nile, in the aisle of airplanes, on the deck of cruise ships, in offices and shops and in the fields.

Washing certain parts and areas of the body with water is in order before prayers. Everyone who possibly can get to water does this, but sometimes water is just not available in the desert. In this situation, rubbing oneself with sand is acceptable for cleansing.

In this electronic age this type of prayer call probably could be replaced with something more technological, but the prayer call is an important part of the culture and Egypt just would not be Egypt without the five times daily call—loud as it is. In order for the *muezzin* to be heard above all the other sounds, he now uses an electronic microphone to call to the people, eliminating the necessity of climbing to the top because the speakers already up there point in four directions. At times it seems to me that each mosque vies for the loudest speakers.

First time visitors to Egypt are often jolted awake by the early morning call, and being unable to understand the Arabic language, some find it rather annoying. Others find the idea behind the call to be quite pleasant. It cannot be avoided. It seems there is a mosque on every corner.

As for me, I sleep through this first call as do most people who choose not to get out of bed at that hour. But I like to be reminded five times every day to slow down, stop what I'm doing and acknowledge my own beliefs.

Often there are special rites at the mosques that are broadcast to all the villages, such as the *dhikar,* a ritual which involves loud rhythmic chanting and repetitive trance-inducing sounds.

What more often awakens me is the early morning braying of the donkey. The donkey is still a very important animal here in Egypt and he often makes that known by his braying. There is no way I can even begin to describe the sound of a donkey braying. Just be assured that it is not like any other sound we know and it is *very* loud. The braying may go on for a good length of time. Hearing this sound for the first time, one would not suspect that it is coming from a donkey.

I'm sure it is the braying of the donkey that awakens the rooster that starts crowing to awaken the lady chicks in his harem. Here in Egypt, the chicken house is rarely on the ground. Most people who keep chickens keep them on the rooftop. Often there are other animals on the rooftop also. Here rooftops are flat and are an extension to the living quarters. Sometimes a few goats or sheep and ducks or geese make their home up there. I have seen a milk cow on the rooftop, but that is not common. Most domestic animals are fed table scraps from the family kitchen along with their diet of *barsem.*

Most of the sounds that are usually confined to inside the house are routinely heard outside; either on the rooftop or in the family courtyard, as much of village living is out-of-doors. The women greet one another from roof to roof and discuss the approaching day, very young children cry or scream for attention, school age boys and girls can't find their belongings, all things considered a normal day.

In the street a vendor selling fresh vegetables and fruit goes along the narrow lane between houses describing his specials for the day into his loud microphone, a device that screeches and screams because it is cheap and old. As the village women gather around his donkey-pulled cart, their voices rise as they greet each other again. The donkey is aware of another donkey in the vicinity and he brays to announce his greetings. The vendor calls out again, just in case someone didn't hear him the first few times and the microphone screeches and screams again. More than one vendor will certainly ply his trade in these lanes, so this scenario may be repeated several times each day. All the while the chickens cackle, the roosters crow, the ducks quack, the birds continue to sing and the dogs bark at nothing that I can see.

One welcome sound usually comes early in the morning and that is the call of the man selling "*fuul.*" *Fuul* is the word for beans, the traditional and typical and delicious breakfast food. The fava beans have been slow cooking in their specially shaped giant pot, out-of-doors, over hot coals all night. This cooking pot is a large round stainless steel bowl, fire-blackened and dented, with a four or five inch diameter straight spout coming out of the top of the bowl. A long handle dipper is required to dip into the spout, then into the bowl to remove the freshly prepared beans.

When I hear the *fuul* man banging on his large round metal pot, I rush outside to my balcony, which hangs over the street. I place a clean bowl inside my special basket with a very long rope attached at the handle, and then drop it down three stories into the street below, with the required money also inside. He removes the money, fills my bowl and I pull my basket back up to my balcony. I have just purchased our breakfast—always so fresh and effortless on my part and without leaving our apartment. He gives his donkey a verbal signal and they move along to the next customer.

The cooing of the pigeons never stops. In village homes there are small openings near the ceiling for the pigeons to come and go freely. They are clean birds—not associated with the dirt that we in the west credit them with. A rice-stuffed pigeon is a delicacy at meal time, though it does not provide a very hearty serving of flesh. When Omran's mother serves meat to the family, she prepares for me a stuffed pigeon, as I avoid eating red meat as much as possible.

An elderly man in the next village died early this morning and he must be buried before sunset today. The best way to spread this news and advise everyone to attend the funeral and/or visit the family to show respect, is to go through each village with a hand-held megaphone or electric microphone blaring this important information over and over again. The announcement must be loud enough to be easily heard over the other sounds.

Any other news or advertisement deemed important will be handled in the same manner. There could be two or three such messages on any given day. The messenger usually rides on a donkey cart or in the back of a pick-up truck. The donkey cart is much more practical because it can enter the narrow lanes where a truck cannot go.

All homes in Egypt use a cylinder of gas for cooking. The cylinder is connected to the *butujaz* (cook stove) inside the house. When the cylinder becomes empty, it must be replaced immediately, so it is important to hear the *embubba* man as he comes around on his donkey cart with large metal gas filled cylinders, stacked in a high pyramid shape.

Because they look like bombs, the Egyptians call them embubba. The driver of this cart sits on top of the gas filled cylinders, smoking his cigarettes, calling out in a grand voice and banging loudly on one of the metal cylinders with his large metal wrench. Later he uses this tool when he connects the *embubba* to the cooker inside the family home. He makes a lot of noise as he traverses the village, but his presence is very necessary and the sound is most welcome.

A young man wanders through the village guiding his herd of sheep or goats as they constantly communicate with each other. If the animals do not continuously converse, one of them risks getting separated from the herd. If there is any cause for alarm amongst the sheep, the volume of their distress increases dramatically as each one warns the others.

I have not mentioned the incessant car horns that never stop. All the while, the motorcycles go through the village, making as much noise as possible. They could be ridden in a quieter manner, but then not everyone would know they are coming or going. Apparently the cycle itself doesn't make enough noise for the rider, so he blasts his horn as he motors along the streets and alleyways. Some of the horns have very interesting sounds. One sounded like a freight train roaring down the track. I wasted no time getting out of the way when I heard that one behind me, even though I knew there was no train track for fifteen miles.

Radios constantly blare out the latest tunes and shopkeepers and taxi drivers with a cassette player broadcast recordings of the chanting of the Quran. This is not done quietly, as one might expect, but rather with as much volume as possible. Even inside the home, the television blares. Loudness is written into the script of television programs.

During all this, the prayer call continues at regular intervals. This call lasts about ten to fifteen minutes, depending on the day and the time. The sounds of the family continue from outside the homes.

A new alarm has invaded Egypt: that of the mobile or cellular telephone. As expected, most everyone has at least one mobile phone on their person and the volume is as loud as possible, in keeping with the chosen signal which is designed to be loud. Several of these phones blasting into the atmosphere at once are enough to make one run for cover. Imagine being in a fourteen passenger public transportation van with five or six telephones blasting off at full volume, all at the same time.

On Fridays, the Islamic holy day, worshippers attend noon prayers at the mosque. Hundreds of men chanting prayers aloud in unison is not a quiet event. These prayers are broadcast from the *minaret,* as is the sermon of the day. Now, suppose there are six mosques within hearing range and each one is broadcasting at top volume, at the same time, from inside each mosque. As all sermons sometimes tend to do, these can get quite loud and filled with emotion.

Friday is the one day during the week that children don't attend school, so all the village children are playing in the narrow lanes and they make a lot of noise with their yelling and laughing and crying and screaming—mostly happy noises.

If the day happens to be Thursday, a village wedding will probably be on the schedule. Thursday evening is wedding evening, because it precedes the holy day, Friday, when some residents have a day off work. Weddings are held out of doors, in the street, with live musicians and a vocalist or a disk jockey managing the tunes. If the music is live then it is typical *Sayedee* music and has its very own character and instruments. If it is managed by a disk jockey then it will include pop and other music styles. One guarantee for any type of music: it will be loud. Egyptians are fond of the triple echo sound, which makes everything three times louder but not easily understood. The volume will be set so high that the music is distorted.

Many brides-to-be observe "The Night of the Henna," on Wednesday before the wedding and this usually involves the same type of music. The music can sometimes be heard in the next village. But there is colorful dancing out of doors and everyone is ready to have a lot of fun on this evening.

A custom that accompanies village weddings is the parade of automobiles full of singing, ululating, clapping, yelling women and loud music and dancing men. Some of the men dance on top of the vans as they move along. These parades are navigated in the most erratic and dangerous manner as they take the bride and groom through the villages. Of course, auto and motorcycle horns are always blaring.

One can expect to hear the women *ululating,* the high pitch trilling sound made by rapidly moving the tongue back and forth against the roof of the mouth. Anytime a woman wishes to show emotion, whether positive or negative, she *ululates* (also called the *zaghreet*) and then her fellow villagers join in. Women make this sound when a baby is born or when a person dies, when a loved one leaves home or when the loved one returns. It's a most spine tingling sound when someone dies and the women come together to let the village know this news. At that time, all the women, dressed in head to toe black, move toward the home of the newly deceased and surround the house, pacing slowly, and give forth with this sound for days—the sad sound. You hear this always at weddings and engagement parties—the happy sound. Imagine the airport waiting and reception areas. When the television shows that the home team makes a goal, you hear it coming from every building.

Each sound I have described is not happening alone. They are all going on in unison. Were any citizen of Egypt to visit the western world, I suspect they would be very annoyed by the sounds and noises that I am comfortable with: power lawn mowers, leaf and snow blowers, police and fire sirens or airplanes and helicopters flying over.

Mud Brick Home

M ost houses in Upper Egyptian villages are very much alike. Egyptians are not adventuresome or creative and seem to have no desire to do something in an individual manner. It's most important to do everything "as we have always done it."

One home I know is a perfect example of an old Egyptian mud brick home. Once upon a time it was possibly the largest and stateliest in the village, but now it is quite the opposite; time and lack of funds have taken their toll. The unpainted cracked walls create sort of a spider web appearance and I often think they might lean just a little to the south. Most homes today have electricity but if the home is constructed of mud, then running water is out of the question; therefore there is no plumbing. Ceilings are very high with open vents to let the heat escape. A mud brick home is somewhat cool and comfortable in the unbearable heat of the Egyptian summer. The open upper vents also serve as passageways, allowing the pigeons to go in and out freely.

In this typical two-story family home there is no kitchen, sink, water, cabinets, table, and no countertop. The cooking area is in a large windowless room with dirt walls and a floor of the same, but this house does have a small butane gas stove standing alone at one end of the room and a small bare light bulb dangling from the ceiling. Some of the best tasting food I've eaten in Egypt came out of cooking areas like this.

One must be careful where one steps or a chicken or duck, pigeon, rabbit, or kitten might be injured. Their home is inside the house also and usually they want to be where the food is. When no person is around, I'm sure it is filled with hungry rats and mice, looking for a meal, but I haven't seen any. The numerous housecats do a good job, but just to be safe, I make a lot of noise if I enter alone.

Scraps, such as potato peels and leftovers, are just tossed on the ground and eaten quickly by the waiting animals. So, you see, a perfect cycle is created, with each action serving a purpose and being necessary in order for the next action to happen. For the fowl, they provide eggs for our table and then they clean up the cooking scraps which are disposed of on the floor. The birds grow into healthy adults and eventually become nutrition for the family, starting the cycle all over again.

There are no plates or silverware to contend with. All food is eaten with good fresh homemade bread. The cook squats and uses any part of the dirt floor as her work area. Water is provided in the undecorated natural clay jugs carried from the outside hydrant or village well.

Prepared food is placed on a large thirty-six inch round tray and carried into another room where everyone sits on the floor, circled around the tray which also sits on the floor, and enjoys eating from common dishes, using their own hands as utensils. Some homes have a short legged, round wooden table which they bring out at mealtime to hold the tray. One family I dine with often cannot afford the special table, so at mealtime they roll a dusty old spare tire into the room and the food tray rests on that. When with this family it became my job to be sure this spare tire was in its proper place when it was time for the tray to appear.

If it's a family meal, then everyone sits together. If there are guests present, two trays will be set up, probably in two different rooms—if the house has two rooms. Or it could be that the men eat first and then the women and children arrive and eat what is left. This is part of the culture of Upper Egypt and may not be practiced *exactly* in this manner in all areas of the country.

When the meal is finished, the tray is picked up and carried away and the room is instantly restored to its pre-meal condition. There really is no "clean-up," as you can see. Pots or clear tea glasses are "washed" with a swirl or two of cold water, which is then sprinkled onto the dirt floor to keep the dust down. If necessary, they will be soaked as needed.

There is no plumbing inside, but at this home, not far from the front door is a small fired brick building standing in the garden, just large enough to house a "squat" type toilet and a cold water shower. This building, with it's piped-in running water, is very satisfactory and feels quite luxurious to the family living here.

Littered all about the room are things a westerner would put out for the trash—broken pieces of furniture, old clothes, an old suitcase, unused pots, newspapers, etc. There is no trash or garbage pick-up nor public dumping ground. I want to emphasize that I have never been inside an Egyptian home that was not clean and odor free. Though it may *sound* questionable, Egyptians are very clean people.

I have not tried to paint a bleak picture; just the opposite. One thing I try to constantly remember here is that people of every culture in the world do what is best for them. When I see how every action feeds from and leads to the next action, I marvel. What works for us in the west will not necessarily work for someone else. And the opposite holds true. Related to this, an Egyptian once told me "We are all content in our own chaos; it's the other people's chaos we can't deal with."

Those who live here are very proud of their family home and they don't hesitate to invite any guest for a meal, meager as it may be. I never hesitate to enjoy sharing a lunch or dinner here, and there have been many. Everyone is healthy and happy and isn't that what we all strive for?

The colorless earthen floors and walls and coolness of the mud brick house provide the perfect environment for snakes—it's just like home for them. We can get comfortable with the mice, rats, geckos, scorpions and other critters running about inside, but a snake in the house does not provide any level of comfort.

When the snake man goes through the village, stopping at every house, he tells each woman that there are snakes hiding in her home and that God has sent him to clean them all out, he usually strikes a business deal. The snake man never fails to find at least one good size snake hiding in a corner of the home or under a bed or in a pile of dirty clothes tossed on the floor. When the hunter pulls this big reptile out of its hiding place with a flourish, appearing to be in grave danger, and shows it to the lady-of-the-house, she is ever so grateful. All during his search he is quoting the Quran and calling upon *Allah*. Of course, the story that follows this man is that he already has the snake in his pocket or stuffed up the sleeve of his cotton *galabaya* when he arrives. Never-the-less, it's a bit of village lore that the women can't risk ignoring.

Fresh Fruit & Veggies

It appears that there is a fresh fruit and vegetable stand on every street corner and at least two in between. There is never any excuse to not eat the freshest of fruits and veggies. My personal policy is that I eat what is in season right here in my area. If it is not grown in my own backyard, figuratively speaking, I don't want it. I like the idea that my produce was probably picked yesterday—or possibly this morning.

I use the same vendor regularly because I get better deals if he knows me and likes me. He puts an extra piece or two into my bag, or he picks out only the best of his supply for me. Often he tells me to wait until tomorrow for a better deal and he cuts the fruit in half so I can see and taste it before purchasing.

Here in Egypt, mangos can grow to almost football size, yet the cantaloupes and honeydews are the size of a small orange. They just melt in my mouth!

It's the custom here to take a gift of fresh fruit when visiting someone's home.

Bathing Brown Blossoms

When the wind blows hard across the desert, the sky gets dark. The blowing sand can block out the sunlight, in addition to rearranging the landscape. I am surrounded by the *sahara* and after a fierce windstorm I can sweep up a bucket full of sand from inside my home.

Today I wanted a bouquet of fresh flowers for inside the house. In the garden, I cut from the pink oleander tree and the white oleander tree, only to discover that the blossoms are now brown, the color of the desert sand. This is the first time I've found it necessary to bathe the sand and dirt off the blossoms and leaves, with soap and water, before arranging them for indoors.

The word *sahara* is the Arabic word meaning desert. So therefore, it is not necessary to say Sahara Desert. Just one of those words is sufficient.

Peanut Butter

At three a.m. Omran received a phone call from a friend, about to leave Hurgada, a resort city on Egypt's Red Sea, and drive to Luxor, about four hours across the Eastern Desert. The friend remembered that I had said I can buy peanut butter at a particular store in Hurgada. This guy had a very generous heart but he had no idea what peanut butter was and he asked me for an Arabic translation. Well, there is none, but I could break down the word. Of course, "butter" is that white stuff that we spread on bread, coming from the rich milk of a water buffalo called *zibda*, and "peanut" translates to *"fuul sudani"* or beans from the south. Miracle of miracles, I received two jars of peanut butter—imported from France.

Taxi

One of the things I like about Egyptians is their keen sense of humor. They particularly like poking fun at their government, and oftentimes at themselves.

Walking alone along a remote deserted road near the temple of Medinet Habu on Luxor's west bank, I saw an old man riding his donkey coming toward me. As he got within hearing range, he looked at me in a very inviting way, and with a twinkle in his eye, he patted the space behind him on the donkey's rump and said to me "Taxi?"

Biblical Land

In some books I've read, Egypt is often referred to as the "Biblical land." My own interpretation of that is because Egypt has the same appearance today as the pictures from the Bible story books of my childhood, this country could easily be related to "biblical." It may also be because Egypt is mentioned around ninety times in the Bible. It could also be because Egypt was a Christian country for about four hundred years, both before and after the Arab invasion.

I've traveled in other Middle Eastern countries with the same cultural background, but most of them have made more advances. The face of Egypt has not changed significantly in hundreds of years, especially here in Upper Egypt.

The Bible stories I learned as a child can well be imagined here. When I'm on the rooftop, I can visualize the hole being cut through the mud roof so that the sick man could be lowered down inside the house where Jesus was healing others. I've "seen" Joseph with Mary on the back of a donkey. Today's traditional Egyptian men's clothing is perhaps the same as that worn by the *fellahin* (peasants) two thousand years ago. Egypt, more than any other Middle Eastern country where I've traveled, has more of this ancient appearance, especially in the rural villages of Upper Egypt.

The Donkey Ride

Four of my western women friends wanted the adventure of riding donkeys over the mountain separating Hatshepsut's Temple and the Valley of the Kings. It's a very scenic excursion; from high on the desert mountain, looking across the major ancient temples and tourist sites, to the green fields beyond, then on to the River Nile. I was the only one in the group who had done this trip a number of times, both on donkey and on foot, so they asked me to arrange it all and to lead them along the correct trails.

At the last minute, when the reality of what we were about to do sunk in, Omran decided he should go with us and he appointed himself "leader." It's a good thing he did! On the very top of the mountain, one of the women fell off her donkey and cracked a rib. She could not walk and she could not ride and we could not carry her. In her extreme pain, we had to get her and the animal down the steep and very narrow mountain trail and back to our base. Underfoot the rocks and sand were loose, allowing for much sliding and slipping and loss of balance. We somehow managed to get her down the mountainside—with the help of three young Egyptian men who appeared from nowhere, it seemed—and the story ended well enough. Once we got off the mountain, we hailed a passing vehicle for we still had about three miles to travel before reaching the hospital. Thankfully, our friend healed beautifully and her donkey ride was probably much more memorable than she wanted. Our planned two hour trip consumed six hours of our day.

Rain

Shocked by the abrupt sharp and very loud noise, I bolted out of bed, awakening as I did so. It sounded like thunder! Running outside into the darkness of the desert, I slipped in a damp spot on the ground. Droplets fell from the sky. I raised my arms to the heavens and just rejoiced that I was seeing and feeling something very familiar: rain drops.

The amount of droplets would not stop a ballgame or a picnic in most places, but here in the desert, it is quite a different feeling. I've read that rain comes to this part of the desert about every seventy-five years. A real rain, that is—not the few drops we experienced. That means that many people can live their entire life and never see rain. Surely, I'm guessing it might rain a little more frequently than seventy-five years, but however often it happens, it is a very rare event.

When I went to visit a friend who was leaving the next day to begin his three-year army duty, he told me he was "really scared." In my most empathetic manner, I agreed that leaving home, family and village for the first time *is* very frightening, and then offered him some comforting words. "No, no, no," he exclaimed. "That's not why I'm scared. I'm going to Alexandria, and they tell me that water falls from the sky there." Well, if I've never seen water falling from the sky, my imagination would go wild as to how that might happen. Here, in the desert of Egypt, rain is often described as "a river in the sky."

Parcels on Top of the Head

The easiest way for a woman to carry a heavy load is to carry it on top of her head. Often my friend Jamalat carries loads on her head that cause her daughter and me together to strain and groan when lifting them up to her.

One day recently I saw a woman walking along the dirt road leading to the ferry with an old, extremely heavy metal washing machine on her head. She had it perfectly balanced and walked with her arms at her sides, in that same elegant stride all women use. I wonder how far she had walked.

I did note that it took three men to lift it off her head so that she could board the ferry. I dreaded to think of her climbing the three flights of stairs to get from river level to street level once she reached the other side of the river.

I keep telling myself that I'm going to learn to carry parcels on top of my head as my Egyptian friends do. The walk of the women here is very elegant and graceful, with their shoulders straight and their head held erect. They have a particular gait to their step that matches their graceful posture. It is the same posture and walk that I tried to master as a teenager in charm school, with a book sliding off the top of my head.

Women can often be seen walking through the village with a three-foot diameter tray, laden with hot cooked food, balanced perfectly, so that nary a drop escapes.

One amusing sight is women walking home after shopping at the market, with a head of cabbage balanced on top of their own head. Cabbage heads here grow to twenty inches diameter and are rather leafy. It looks like a big fluffy hat, something like one I used to own.

Men don't often carry heavy loads on top of their heads. Men carry extremely heavy loads on their back while bending over. However, I do see construction workers climbing ladders with large containers of wet cement on their heads. In Cairo I saw a man riding his bicycle through the horrific traffic, balancing a gleaming white wedding cake on a tray on his head. Worse yet, there was no cover on the cake to ward off the foul, dirty air.

Old Wives Tales

One of the reasons that old wives tales prevail is due to the lack of education of the population. They are amusing to me and I often try to place some logic in some of them, but so far, to no avail.

We arrived at the home of my husband's sister so that we could offer her daughter our congratulations on the birth of her new baby and to welcome the newborn into the world with a gift. As Omran opened the door to enter the house, he was stopped by much shouting out orders to not enter the house. He was instructed to go back outside and re-enter backward, including coming down the steps. The reason being: if he had seen meat hanging on the hook on his way to the house, the mother's milk would dry up and she would not be able to nurse the baby. Entering the house backwards would prevent this situation. It is very possible he could have seen this because butcher shops hang animal carcasses outside in the fresh air and sunshine, the blowing sand and auto exhaust; all in the path of passing pedestrians.

Another time I had the same greeting when going to visit a new baby. I did not know the mother of the child, but I had been invited by her sister. The reason I had to enter backward, I was told, is that if the new mother saw me face forward in our first meeting, she would not be able to have more children.

A woman was stressing to me and a doctor friend that her daughter had been married for nearly a year and had not yet conceived a child. This woman was certain that if her daughter would lay her eyes upon a dead person and pull the sheet over the face, that she would then become pregnant. She wanted confirmation from the doctor that this would be successful. Of course, my friend, the doctor made no guarantees.

Finally, a couple weeks later her daughter got the opportunity to pull the sheet over a dead body. I'll be watching to see if the daughter becomes pregnant. The positive belief that she will become pregnant *could* be a factor that makes it happen.

One custom that didn't take much to figure out had to do with eggplants. When going to visit another newborn, I noted that above every doorway there was an eggplant nailed to the door frame. The purpose of this is to insure that the mother's milk comes in plentifully. You will note that most eggplants have the shape of a full breast.

I was informed that if a pregnant woman isn't given the very foods she craves or wants during pregnancy, it will show up on the skin of her newborn child. Omran has a small mole on his shoulder which is attributed to his mother's wanting, but not receiving, *falafel* during her pregnancy. One of his sisters has a birthmark; the result of her mother craving, but not getting, liver to eat during this time.

One particularly nice custom here centers on childbirth. When a woman is about to deliver a baby, she goes to the home of her mother, or her family home, and stays for forty days. If she already has little ones, they also go along to grandma's house, where everyone is well cared for. However, if this is her eighth or ninth delivery, Mama comes to her. She has plenty of help while convalescing. Her husband can visit her during this time, but it is clear that this is a woman's world.

Until very recently all newborns and infants were wrapped in swaddling clothes; nothing more than rags or torn up adult clothing. Shops did not carry items for babies so I made a practice of keeping cuts of soft flannel on hand and I made a tiny *galabaya* for each new born I visited. In Egypt there is no tradition of pink and blue or pastel colors for babies and the only flannel I could buy was bright lime green with orange designs on it. Mothers were thrilled! Most times this little *galabaya* was the only new item for the new baby.

Trip to Luxor

When Omran and I were living on the desert's edge, beyond the Valley of the Kings, in a small village reasonably near his home village on the west side of the Nile, I needed a thimble for sewing and I needed to mail a letter. This meant a trip to town: Luxor. First I walked a mile, and then stood by the road until I saw a doorless van or a canvas canopied pick-up truck coming my way. I flagged down this public transportation, quickly climbed in, and we headed toward the River Nile, a distance of about six miles, picking up and dropping passengers along the way.

There were always four or five men and boys standing on the rear bumper, galabayas filled with air and blowing in the wind. It seems to be the macho way for the young guys to travel, even when seats are available.

At the river, I left the public pick-up truck and boarded the ferry (no bridges here) for the crossing—always a relaxing and pleasurable experience. Once on the other side in Luxor, I walked about twenty minutes to find another public transportation, this time a fourteen passenger van, with the passenger door permanently fixed open as people continuously come and go. There are no designated stopping places; one just stands at the side of the road or street and signals the driver when a van comes along. When the driver stops or slows down, I call out my destination and if he is going my way, he tells me to get in. If not, he drives on and I begin the process all over again.

There's no receptacle in which to drop the fare. The passenger seats himself immediately, and then hands his fare to the passenger in front of him, who hands it to the person in front of him, etc., until it reaches the driver. When passing the fare along, it is important to say a number—how many fares this amount is intended for. That way, when the money reaches the driver, he knows if he should send change back—in the same manner.

The driver controls the money. Somehow through his rear view mirror he knows who has paid and who has not. I've never witnessed anyone trying to avoid paying. The driver counts the money and makes and distributes the change, all while darting through the fast moving traffic, the children in the streets, and the many pedestrians, bicycles and donkey carts.

When I'm ready to get out of the van, I just call out in Arabic, "Stop here, please." In the towns, these vehicles run bumper to bumper, literally, and they are always full.

After mailing my letter from a special communication shop, I got into another van for the trip to the *suq* (market place). I was on a mission this day so I resisted the temptation to look at other items, although the *suq* is always a colorful and fun place to be. Buying a thimble doesn't take long, and I was now ready to reverse everything I had just done and head back home, exactly like I came.

Total time: just under three hours. Total transportation cost: three Egyptian pounds or fifty cents U.S. Cost to mail special letter: thirty dollars U.S. Cost of thimble: seven Egyptian or just over one dollar U.S. (A regular letter from Egypt to U.S. takes about thirty days, if it makes it at all. This letter needed to be in the U.S. in three to five days, so was sent via special courier.) Not counting the cost of mailing the letter, I had spent one dollar and fifty cents.

As I walked the last part of my journey back home, I stopped for take away food for my dinner. I bought from a man standing in the dirt and dust beside the road—with a portable butane cooker—making and selling *falafel* and Egyptian pickles. There was no roof overhead, no table or chair, no running water, no electricity. Total cost, enough for two meals: two Egyptian pounds or about thirty-five cents U.S.

Best part of the entire trip: being on the River Nile and watching the magnificent red-orange sunset! Long before I reached my home, darkness had set in.

I am often asked by people in the U.S. if Egypt is safe and what about safety for women? Would I venture out alone, on foot, returning after dark, in the U.S. to make the trip described above? Would I venture out at ten at night to walk to the vegetable stand, about half mile on a narrow lonely road by the light of the moon? In the U.S. would Omran's immediate family of four women and a child feel comfortable sleeping outdoors in the front courtyard for three quarters of the year? Never have I been alarmed or frightened.

Scorpions

As I sat at the outdoor table in a friend's garden, calmly sipping my tea, I looked down and saw that I had just inadvertently stepped on and killed a scorpion—before it had an opportunity to attack me. The color drained from my face and my knees felt weak. Because I wasn't stung, I joyously declared, *il hamdu lil Allah*.

Scorpion history in Egypt goes back to ancient times when they were considered both frightening and dangerous and they were also worshipped as a goddess and protector. In fact, scorpions have been on earth over four hundred million years. The beautiful ancient Egyptian goddess, Selket, is often shown wearing a gold scorpion as her crown. She was a goddess of magic, and magic was a major part of the healing process in ancient times.

The scorpions I've seen measured from three inches up to six inches in their body length. Their venom-filled stinger which curls upward like a tail ready to strike, adds an additional three to four inches. They have frontal claws which gives them somewhat the appearance of a crab. The venom causes more deaths than Egypt's dangerous snakes. Only about fifty species of scorpions worldwide have venom capable of killing a human, and at least one of those species makes its home in Egypt.

Late one night as I sat at home alone, deeply concentrating and writing in my journal, from the corner of my eye I saw something moving swiftly across the floor, coming directly toward me. It was a big scorpion. I prepared to attack it before it attacked me. Had I been able to safely remove it from the house to the desert out of doors, I would have done so, but I felt I had no choice but to kill it. It *could* kill me!

If I stomped on it, the scorpion could easily flip his stinger up and put it right into my foot. So I chose to remove my shoe and use it to beat the scorpion till dead.

Not wanting to lose my train of thought, I quickly returned to my writing, telling myself that I will clean up the dead scorpion later. After all, it wasn't going anywhere now. Later, when I turned my thoughts again to the scorpion, it was invisible; covered with millions of minute black ants, and ants still marching in under my door from the desert. An army of them.

What a dilemma! It would have been so much easier to toss out the dead scorpion rather than to deal with millions of hungry feasting ants. I knew I couldn't sweep them up into the dustpan and I had no such thing as a vacuum cleaner. I certainly didn't want them to spread throughout my house. There was no way I could remove the ants without them taking over my body as they had taken the scorpion's body. Some floors in Egypt are made of ceramic tile and unharmed by water. I boiled two large kettles of water, stood on a chair beside and above the dead scorpion and feasting ants and drowned the little critters in a cascade of boiling water. That wasn't the way I wanted this saga to end, but I felt I had no choice. Of course, then I had to clean all the floors.

Omran's teenage nephew was stung on the thigh by a scorpion, and he was rushed to the hospital and given a dose of anti-venom. After a few days of bed rest, this healthy young man was ready to be up and limping about.

When my mother-in-law put her hand into a jar, she screamed in pain and we all knew she had been stung by a scorpion. Omran rushed her to the hospital, where she received an injection of anti-venom from the doctor and was sent home for prescribed bed rest.

Many villagers, particularly the elderly, have more faith in the village healer and his folk medicine than in doctors and modern medicine. Rather than going directly home after her hospital visit, *Om Gozi* wasted no time getting to the village healer to treat the scorpion bite on her hand. Upon examination, the healer took a razor blade, wiped the dust and dirt off on his sleeve, and then proceeded to make a few cuts in his patient's hand.

Then with a regular drinking glass and using a single piece of paper he made a fire inside the glass. He picked up the heated glass with his bare fingers, turned the glass upside down over the freshly made cuts, and held it firmly in place. The vacuum created by this action caused the glass to fill with the poisoned blood coming from the bite area. The healer gives all credit to *Allah* and the *Quran* as he continually prays and recites from the Holy Book during this entire operation. *Om Gozi* healed beautifully.

Clinic Volunteer

Two days a week I donate my afternoon to a clinic for mentally and physically handicapped children. I'm learning a lot! One of the things that is very obvious and really stands out is how much these children are loved. Few of these patients can walk and must be carried, so a family member brings each one to the clinic. Carrying a thirteen year old young man is not an easy task for his older sister or brother.

I have long noticed that handicapped persons are graciously and lovingly accepted by society here. There is so little available for people of this nature and it seems to me that every little gesture is very much appreciated. As these children grow, and it becomes impossible to carry them, I wonder if they will have opportunities to go outside their homes in their later years. The clinic itself is on the second and third floors of the building, with only cement stairs to lead the way.

It is very rare to see adults or youth in wheel chairs or scooters or any of the other conveniences and aids that are very common in the west. There are no special services available for this type of equipment; no ramps, no elevators or escalators, but many broken and pot-holed sidewalks and streets.

Mubarak's Downfall, Egypt's Uprising

As I was beginning to settle into my chair to write my thoughts and feelings about the events of the day, I heard a lot of shouting in the street below my third floor flat, in the town of Luxor. A group of young men were hurrying along the street carrying clubs and big sticks and making a loud racket. I never did learn what that was all about, even though we hurriedly dressed and hit the streets of town ourselves. We expected to see all the same things we had been witnessing on the television from Cairo, but alas, there was none of that.

Though the young men with the clubs were the most disruptive thing we experienced or witnessed during the last five days, they were peaceful and orderly—just noisy. Every day we have been on the streets—completely aware that Egypt is under a curfew—but people pay about the same amount of attention to a curfew as they pay attention to traffic rules and regulations. We have seen the aftermath of a few broken storefronts here in Luxor and heard of things being stolen. We remain transfixed in front of our television watching the events taking place in Cairo and Alex.

Here in Luxor an atmosphere of peace prevails. At this time I have no fears for my own safety or the safety of any Upper Egyptian. I have complete confidence that I will be protected and cared for by my Egyptian family and friends.

For seven days we have had no internet, no air travel, and no gasoline for the vehicles. Our cell phone service has just been restored (the government also shut that down) and we can occasionally find an ATM that works, but requests that we take no more than one thousand Egyptian pounds—that's approximately one hundred-sixty U.S. dollars. Banks and schools are closed. Food is getting scarce. Airplanes are grounded and airports are closed; trains and busses are not operating. Cairo's Metro is stopped. The American Embassy is closed and I have not had any success in trying to contact them via telephone or internet.

The ferry to cross the Nile here at Luxor is working sporadically. We went to the west bank but had to hire a private motor launch to return to Luxor. It is no fun crossing the Nile at midnight on a moonless, starless night with no lights on our boat or any other boat on the river. For a while there was no police or army presence. Many citizens feel safer when there is no government authority about. Shops and *suqs* are closed.

I keep hearing rumors of looting and I am going on the assumption this is all true. Even on the west bank I hear of government properties being vandalized. There are still tourists in town because they have no way to leave.

Egyptian television is government owned so they have blocked much of the coverage from Egypt. We have been watching Al Jazeera television but last night the government kicked them out, arrested their reporters, and tried to confiscate their cameras. Coverage from CNN is still available and I have been using that as my news source. Omran prefers to watch everything in his language and, of course, I prefer to watch everything in my language, so that's the way we do it. Then we explain to each other and compare the facts—at least, the media calls it that.

CNN tells me that the USA has sent an airplane to evacuate American citizens.

I have seen television coverage of the Cairo airport, and if planes were taking off, there would be no way for me to get to Cairo, with trains not running either. If trains were operating, it is a twelve-hour trip (on a good day!) and then I would need to cross the city, going past the demonstration area of Tahrir Square. Should I be fortunate enough to reach the airport, the television cameras show me there is not space for one additional person. Further, I can't reach anyone by phone or internet who can tell me when this plane is scheduled to depart, if there is space available, or where is its destination or what is the cost.

After announcing the country's transportation closures, and the closure of the airport, the closure of the Embassy and the internet, CNN instructed us Americans to contact the airlines or the American Embassy and to go on-line. Crazy! So I made the decision to stay in Luxor. I feel this is the safest position for me right now, but that could change in an instant. I recorded this on January 29, 2011.

Calling the Young Men

A few months ago we moved from the desert house on the west side into a third floor apartment in Luxor, directly above the neighborhood mosque. Early yesterday evening I heard the imam making an announcement over the speaker system. He was calling all the neighborhood young men to the mosque, saying they need to make a plan for the safety of the neighborhood, as there is the possibility of breaking and looting. The men came streaming out of their homes and into the mosque as if they were answering a meal call.

Later in the evening I felt very safe and secure, seeing these handsome young men, gathered in groups of four to six and positioned all along our street, carrying big sticks, clubs and in some instances, knives. I'm quite sure they held their positions until morning. There were no incidents in this neighborhood!

All across Egypt the people are protecting their own property and families—feeling more confident doing it themselves rather than expecting the police or army to do it. But now there is no active army or police force. I hope that soon some sort of reasonable law can be re-established here in Luxor.

A Peaceful Day in Luxor

On television Omran and I watched President Mubarak's resignation speech, giving up his thirty year dictatorial rule over the Egyptian people. Then we watched the extremely disruptive aftermath of that speech in Tahrir Square in Cairo and other major Egyptian cities—almost unable to believe our eyes and ears. We dressed and went out for tea and *shisha* just the same as we do every day. Nothing is different. All's quiet here in Luxor. I didn't see any police or army presence. We saw a few small group gatherings in the square behind Luxor Temple and Abu el Haggag Mosque, but they were not any larger than family gatherings. It's difficult to believable that it could be so quiet and peaceful here in Luxor with so much turmoil in other places in Egypt.

This day was such a pleasant and quiet day. I went to the west bank after lunch and visited with Egyptian friends, then met my Canadian girlfriend for girl talk and tea. Later, I called on Ahmed, good friend and owner of the Amon Hotel, and then met Omran who came over on the boat, bringing a group of six musicians. One of his cousins was hosting a party on his rooftop, and of course that was next on our to-do list. It was a good party—everybody danced every dance and the musicians were great.

Such wonderful memories are produced from evenings like this. I wish there was a way to capture the scene. A lot of private parties are on the rooftops of homes. Upon arrival the six Sayeede musicians removed their shoes, folded their legs up under themselves and began playing their native music non-stop. The moon and stars were out in full force and the reflection of lights on the Nile was breathtaking. From up high on the roof top we could look across the River and right into the magnificent Luxor Temple on the east side.

The internet is back. I hope it stays.

This entire experience has been one of wonder for me. Having devoted so much time to studying Egypt's four thousand years of history, to find myself so close to the making of it now feels quite miraculous. But this is the second time I have been a witness to history here—in 1997 when the horrible massacre of 58 tourists happened on the west bank I was right here in Luxor.

Life continues at a normal pace for us. I am sad for the rest of the country.

I recorded this on Feb. 12, 2011

Muslim Brotherhood

Eighty-three years ago the world's oldest and largest Islamic political group was established in Egypt: The Muslim Brotherhood. Many say it is the most powerful group in Egypt, and it is certainly the most active, though that activity appeared very quiet during the years of former President Mohamed Hosni Mubarak. Mubarak outlawed the existence of the Brotherhood, had known members arrested and jailed, and did not allow members to run for political office, just to name of few of the restrictions.

During the January 2011 revolution the Muslim Brotherhood was active but kept a very low profile. Now that individuals are experiencing the freedom to publicly proclaim their allegiance and devotion to this organization, it appears to me that more and more members are doing so. All over Luxor there are signs and banners announcing a lecture or some other type of gathering, sponsored by the Brotherhood. From what I've been able to determine, these gatherings take the form of pep talks and they are not heavy-handed, there's no condemning any person or organization, and there's a lot of looking forward to a new Egypt.

Either the organization is very quickly growing in numbers or members who previously were forced to be secretive about their affiliation are now coming forward with their attire and other appearance to declare that they are, indeed, members of the Muslim Brotherhood. I see beards appearing on many faces that were previously clean shaven.

One of the things that identify a devout Muslim man, (such as a Brother) is his choice to wear a full beard, usually with a shaved mustache. I fear that to be beardless will set one apart as a non-Brother.

Since the revolution I also notice more women wearing the niqab (face veil), which like the man's beard, symbolizes sincere devotion to Islam and to Allah.

At a Red Sea resort where Omran and I were vacationing there was a man, identified as an ultra-conservative Muslim by his facial hair, along with his wife and young child, lounging at the pool. He was comfortably stretched out on a lounge chair wearing nothing but the typical brief swim trunks while the wife sat on the steps leading down into the pool, playing with their young child. She was adorned in her *black abaya, black hijab, black niqab,* and wearing her *black gloves.* I could see only her eyes—and not much of them. The Quran is very clear in instructing that both men and women must dress modestly, but in my opinion, men have a more relaxed dress code. They are required to cover their body from the knees to the waist.

The Quran tells us that the wives of the prophet were required to cover their faces so men would not think of them in sexual terms. According to tradition, a woman's husband can require her to cover her face if he thinks she is too beautiful and that looking at her might be enticing to the opposite sex.

Like the youth in Egypt who led the revolution, the young men in the Brotherhood are breaking away from some of the organization's traditions and wanting a more prominent role. Some younger women want to be recognized as members and want to be active participants. Some of the deeply religious current members are viewing the Muslim Brotherhood as too liberal while others seek to deepen the role of religion in everyone's life. The organization is known for doing much-needed charity work in Egypt.

It's easy to see why this organization is so controversial. Here in Egypt they are either loved or hated. There's no middle ground. Every Egyptian I have spoken with who is not already a Brotherhood member wants nothing to do with the Brothers. They are adamant about not wanting any one of them elected to public office and they don't want to do business with them.

Many Egyptians don't like the way they call attention to themselves. In addition to the beard, in Upper Egypt they can usually be identified by the white crocheted or embroidered skull cap with a scarf draped over their head in a non-Egyptian style, and their *galabayas* are not traditionally Egyptian style and are usually white in color. It's a uniform, of sorts, and it sets them apart.

This evening I was an observer at a meeting the group held on the plaza behind Abu el Hagagg Mosque here in Luxor. Seeing large numbers of Brothers around this town is something new. This event was well advertised, and I'm sure many in attendance came from other towns. I have attended many events in this plaza, and this had the largest attendance of anything I've seen—except for the Ramadan entertainment.

A large number of veiled women were in attendance, seated all together in a private curtained, secluded area off to the side, in keeping with their traditions. They could not see any of the men in attendance or be seen by any of the men.

There is a lot of speculation that this organization will continue to grow and hopefully, it will balance itself. Currently, reports say the organization has the support of about twenty percent of the Egyptian people, but I have a feeling it is definitely much more. There are branches of the Muslim Brotherhood organization in most major countries of the world, including the United States.

For a period in the not too distant past, The Muslim Brotherhood was quite a militant group and created a lot of problems with their activities. I was afraid to ride the night train from Luxor to Cairo, because passengers were routinely shot at from the outside of the train and some were killed while the train passed through Middle Egypt. Though no one was ever charged, the Brotherhood was suspect, though I don't know if there was legitimate reason for that. Middle Egypt has been a stronghold for the Brotherhood, and it seems they are much quieter now. Peaceful activities are one of their objectives, they now say, and the little bits that I've seen so far uphold that. They have changed the name of their political party to the Freedom and Justice Party.

One of their missions is to establish *Sharia* Law in Egypt and many Egyptians are much opposed to that. However, a number of citizens are strongly in favor of Sharia Law, which is the moral and religious code of Islam. Sharia Law covers just about every aspect of life including conducting business, family matters including inheritance, sexuality, diet and more.

I recorded this on March 15, 2011.

After The Revolution

The things I see changing are not at all what I expected to see.

Here in Luxor, where life goes on at a slow pace, I was surprised to see advertising for a big event called "Egypt Moving Forward." This event was sponsored by local individuals and businesses, both native and foreigners, to promote the return of tourism. It was as it was billed: "a cultural extravaganza and a celebration of new beginnings with professional performances by folkloric dancers, Sufi dancers, pharaoni and Mismar music with stick dancing, Nubian, and Rababa music". Of course, all this was interlaced with the usual pep talks and speeches.

It was well attended. One of the things I enjoy most about events like this is the location. There's a huge plaza behind Luxor Temple and in front of Abu el Haggag Mosque, so these two famous landmarks provide a beautiful scenic background. I know no words that will even allow me to try and describe the sky as the sun sets behind Luxor Temple. I'll just say that if one was not a believer before witnessing this sunset, I'm sure one would be a believer afterward.

Egyptians are fond of using memorable dates as place names; as an example there's 6 October Bridge in Cairo and 6 October City, a newer city created from the desert outside of Cairo. 6 October was the starting date for the war against Israel, which resulted in Egypt reclaiming the Sinai.

A few days ago I noticed a local hotel had changed its name to The New Egypt Hotel and the new coffee house connected to it is now known as 25 January Coffee House, named for the beginning date of the recent demonstrations in Cairo.

On the other hand, I notice a flurry of construction in and around Luxor. Now that there is no government there are no offices to make application for building permits, which often require a lot of red tape, money under the table, and waiting and waiting. Many citizens feel this is the time to start and, hopefully, finish their building projects. Once the building is complete, it could be quite a problem to make the owner tear it down.

Often people who have never experienced freedom and democracy just do not understand these concepts. Some think that freedom means one can do anything one pleases. We were driving down a one-way street in Luxor and encountered a car coming from the wrong direction. When Omran pointed this out to the driver, his response was: "It doesn't matter. We can go anyplace. We can do anything we want to. Now we have freedom."

Enthusiasm runs high and hopes and dreams are revived. Egypt's changes are taking place in a peaceful and purposeful manner. I'm very proud of the Egyptian people, and I pray that their path continues in that way.

I recorded this on March 4, 2011.

Glossary

Abaya—black full length outer garment worn by the women.

Allah—God

Baba—Papa

Baladi—country, native, local

Butujaz—cook stove

Dhikar—religious ceremony

Eid el Adha—religious celebration

Embubba—gas-filled cylinder used mostly for cooking

Falafel—very common food made with ground beans.

Felucca—Nile River boat, used since ancient times

Fuul—beans

Galabaya—full length garment worn by men and women.

Jonna Castle

Ghawah—coffee house

Gozi—my husband

Hijab—to cover head and body in the Islamic style—for women

Hilal moon—crescent moon.

Iftar—Break-the-fast meal.

Il hamdulil Allah—thanks to God

Inshallah—If God wills it. Everything is in the hands of God.

Jidda—grandmother

Minaret—round tower on top of mosque

Mismar—religious celebration

Mulid—celebration for deceased religious man

Muezzin—man who makes the prayer call from mosque

Nana—mint

Niquab—a face cover for women.

Om—mother

Ramadan Karim—Ramadan is generous. Typical Ramadan greeting.

Sabah el Kheir—good morning

Sahara—desert

Sharia law—laws from the Quran

Shisha—waterpipe

Shokran—thank you

Shy—tea

Suq—market place, usually out-of-doors

Ululate or zaghreet—loud shrill sound made by women to express emotion

Yalla—come here, hurry, faster

CPSIA information can be obtained at www.ICGtesting.com
Printed in the USA
BVOW02s0350310813

330021BV00004B/315/P

9 781481 758628